SIMPLY THE BEST
PRESSURE COOKER RECIPES
MARIAN GETZ

INTRODUCTION BY WOLFGANG PUCK
VOLUME 2

AS I LEARNED LONG AGO, ALONGSID
AND GRANDMOTHER, YOU SHOULD
LOTS OF LOVE INTO EVERYTHING YOU
IS CERTAINLY EVIDENT IN THIS COOK

Wolfgang Puck

MOTHER
'S PUT
THIS

Today's generation of pressure cookers are designed to ensure safe and easy cooking. This appliance uses steam pressure to break down the fibers of the food allowing for faster cooking times. Tough meats become tender quickly, vegetables and grains are infused with flavors, and foods retain their nutrients. Although the pressure cooker is mainly used as a timesaving device, it works for fine cooking as well.

When I asked Marian to write the cookbook for the pressure cooker, I knew she would rise to the occasion. Her experience as a pastry chef, wife, mother, and now grandmother allowed Marian to put together a pressure cooker cookbook with a wide variety of recipes that I'm sure you will use for years to come.

A student of cooking is probably one of the best ways to describe Marian. She is always looking for something new, something fresh, something local, something seasonal. Her culinary knowledge combined with her passion for cooking is second to none. The recipes that Marian has written for this cookbook will motivate you to be more creative in the kitchen.

OPEN
CLOSE

COOK WARM

WOLFGANG PUCK

TIMER

PRESSURE COOKER TIPS

Cooking food in your pressure cooker is one of the best time and money-saving methods in the kitchen. Pressure cooking can be up 70% faster than regular cooking and can save up to 70% energy compared to traditional cooking. Foods cooked under pressure get infused with wonderful flavors. As a result, less salt, herbs and spices are necessary which also saves money since herbs and spices can be expensive. In addition, pressure cooking retains more nutrients and essential vitamins in the food. The recipes in this book provide instructions for the most popular pressure cooker sizes, the 5-quart, 6-quart, 8-quart and 10-quart models. Before starting a recipe, determine which size cooker model you own and follow the ingredient suggestion that correlates to your model then proceed to follow the method (which is the same for all models).

MEATS

If you like fall-apart, tender, juicy meats cooked in less than an hour, then the pressure cooker will become a dear friend in your kitchen. The pressure cooker is able to achieve such tender meats in a short time by cooking in a sealed and pressurized environment which causes the temperature inside to rise considerably higher than the normal simmering temperature of 212°F. This is great news for busy cooks who just want to make hassle-free meals that taste good.

VEGETABLES

If you are a vegetarian or vegan, or your doctor is encouraging you to eat more vegetables, then there is no finer way to cook such foods than using a pressure cooker. I pressure cook dried beans as well as dark, leafy greens at least 5 times a week and do it in minutes instead of hours thanks to my pressure cooker. Also, pressure cooked foods retain more vitamins and nutrients than foods cooked on the stove top or oven because they are cooked far more rapidly and in considerably less liquids. If you prefer your vegetables to be firmer, add them to the pressure cooker during the last 5-10 minutes of cooking. To do so, release the pressure manually (see next page for more information), add the vegetables then secure the lid. The pressure cooker will resume cooking for the remaining time.

FROZEN FOOD

If you are adding frozen items to the pressure cooker, you do not need to adjust the cooking time specified in the recipe. The pressure cooker can only come to pressure once the contents boil, so it will take a bit longer to reach pressure but the cooking time should remain the same.

LIQUID

The pressure cooker requires the use of liquid to operate properly. The liquid creates steam which builds up and raises the temperature which is the reason it cooks so fast. If you don't add enough liquid or your liquid is really thick, for example using BBQ sauce by itself, there will not be enough liquid to build steam and the pressure cooker will switch to KEEP WARM mode. If this happens, carefully remove the lid and adjust the liquid accordingly. If you want to try your own recipe creations in the pressure cooker, use this rule of thumb to estimate the liquid needed: Add 1 cup of liquid (water, broth, wine etc.) then add 1/3 cup liquid for every 15 minutes of cooking time. Also, you will notice abbreviations in the ingredient charts for this book. TBSP stands for tablespoon and tsp stands for teaspoon.

COOK ONCE - EAT TWICE

You will love having a pressure cooker, even if you are just cooking for 1 or 2 people. Pressure cooked foods taste even better the next day and freeze beautifully. Divide your cooked food into portions then store in the refrigerator or freezer. This is a great way to have meals just waiting for a too-busy-to-cook day. Any time you can cook once and eat twice you are saving your precious time as well as money.

RELEASING PRESSURE/STEAM NATURALLY

In most cases, especially when pressure cooking meats, it is important to allow the pressure inside the unit to release naturally after cooking. The reason this is so important is that when meat cooks under pressure, the fibers open up and become soft and tender. If you quickly release the pressure manually, the sudden rush of cold air inside the pressure cooker causes those same fibers to tighten up rapidly which will toughen the meat. Please allow the pressure to release naturally after cooking for the most tender food. The time it takes for the pressure to be fully released depends on the amount of food inside the pressure cooker. The more food is inside, the longer it takes. Soups take a long time as well as they are mostly liquid.

RELEASING PRESSURE/STEAM MANUALLY

Some recipes in this book call for the pressure to be released manually. Certain foods such as vegetables do not benefit from natural steam release like meats do so releasing the steam manually helps speed things up. To release pressure manually, unplug the pressure cooker and turn the steam vent to VENT. Use caution when manually releasing the pressure as hot steam will be released. For foods with a lot of liquid such as soups, hot liquid might also be released so natural steam release is recommended. Use tongs, a pot holder or kitchen towel to turn the steam vent.

OVERFILLING

The pressure cooker will not work if you overfill it. There must be enough empty space inside the pressure cooker for the pressure to build. If you overfill the unit, the food will boil instead of cook under pressure. As a general rule, do not fill the unit over 2/3 full or past the MAX fill line as indicated on the inside of the removable cooking pot. For foods that expand during cooking such as rice or dried vegetables, do not fill the unit over 1/2 full. See the manual for additional information.

USE CAUTION

It is very important to always use caution when using the pressure cooker as the steam and condensation can be very hot. Always use a pot holder or kitchen towel when handling the lid, steam vent, removable cooking pot, steaming rack or foil sling. Remember to unplug the appliance before removing the cooking pot.

7

FOIL SLING

If you are baking in the pressure cooker, it can be difficult to add or remove the baking vessel, such as a baking pan, from the pressure cooker. You can fashion a "sling" out of a piece of aluminum foil to help you move the cooking vessel in and out of the pressure cooker. Once you place it in the pressure cooker, tuck the excess foil inside the pressure cooker. Once done cooking, simply lift the foil sling out of the pressure cooker by the handle using a pot holder or towel.

FOIL SLING INSTRUCTIONS

Step 1:
Use a strip of aluminum foil about 20-inches long.

Step 2:
Fold the aluminum foil strip in half lengthwise.

Step 3:
Bring the two ends together then fold the ends tightly to make a "handle".

Step 4:
Place cooking vessel inside the center of the sling.

BROWNING

If you wish to brown or sear foods before pressure cooking, simply turn the timer to any setting which will preheat the pressure cooker similar to a pot on a stove. Add oil or butter then brown your food with the lid off. Once ready to pressure cook, simply secure the lid and reset the timer per the recipe instructions. If you wish to add a brown crust to the cooked food, you can stir in the final ingredients per the recipe then turn the timer back on and cook for a few minutes with the lid off while monitoring the browning with a spatula. Browning the bottom works best for foods that are quite dry such as macaroni and cheese. Very saucy or liquid foods do not tend to brown well.

SALT

The salt used in this book is Diamond Crystal Kosher Salt. It is half as salty as most other brands as the grains are very fluffy and therefore not as many fit into a measuring spoon. If using a different brand of salt, simply use half the amount specified in the recipe or adjust as desired.

VANILLA

I adore vanilla and order both my vanilla extract and vanilla beans from a supplier directly from the island of Tahiti. Tahitian beans and extract are my favorite. I use both of these in recipes where the vanilla takes center stage in flavor. If vanilla is not the star flavor, I use imitation vanilla. It adds the correct taste and aroma without overpowering the stronger flavors in the recipe and is far less expensive. I am also crazy about an inexpensive imitation flavoring called Magic Line Butter Vanilla Extract. It adds an incredible sweet smell and taste to baked goods. Its aroma reminds me of how a really good bakery smells.

BUTTER

All of the butter used in this book is unsalted. Softened butter means butter that has been left at room temperature for several hours. It should be soft enough to offer no resistance whatsoever when sliced with a knife. While there is no substitute for butter's pure flavor, you can use a substitute such as margarine, vegan margarine and coconut oil if necessary. Most of the recipes will turn out fairly well.

SWEETENER

If you need to use a sugar substitute, my favorite kind is an all-natural product called Zsweet. I get it at my local health food store. While it does not bake as perfectly as regular sugar, it is the best substitute I know. My other choice is stevia. I also really like agave syrup, dates as well as honey and use it in many of my recipes if a liquid form of sugar can be used.

MAKING GRAVY

If you prefer for the juices in the pressure cooker to have more of a gravy-like texture, it is really easy to do. Stir a handful of store-bought instant potato flakes into the bubbling juices and stir until you like the texture, adding more if needed. Another way to do this is to mix equal parts of flour and water together then whisk mixture into the bubbling juices until thickened.

COOKING CHART

Below please find the pressure cooker cooking chart for my favorite foods. The chart can be used as a reference for all pressure cooker sizes between 5 and 10 quart.

INGREDIENT	AMOUNT	TIME (MINUTES)	LIQUID SUGGESTED (CUPS)
VEGETABLES, LEGUMES & GRAINS			
Artichokes, trimmed [2]	3 med	12	2
Beans, Black [1]	1 cup	12 ▲	4
Beans, Lima [1]	1 cup	15 ▲	2
Beans, Navy [1]	1 cup	8 ▲	4
Beans, Pinto [1]	1 cup	15 ▲	4
Beans, Red Kidney [1]	1 cup	15 ▲	4
Chick Peas [1]	1 cup	18 ▲	4
Cabbage Head, quartered [2]	1 med	3	2
White Rice, such as Basmati [1]	1 cup	6	1
Brown Rice [1]	1 cup	15	1 cup + 2 TBSP
MEATS & POULTRY			
Beef Brisket [1]	3 lbs	90	2
Pot Roast [1]	3 lbs	35	2
Chicken Breast, boneless, skinless, fresh or frozen [1]	4 lbs	6	2
Chicken Legs [1]	4 whole	20	2
Chicken, quartered [1]	1	20	2
Chicken, whole [1]	3 lbs	20	3
Corned Beef [1]	3 lbs	90	3
Ribs [1]	2 slabs	25	2
Lamb Shanks [1]	2-3 lbs	30	2
Pork Chops (8-10 oz. ea) [1]	3 to 4	12	2
Beef Stew [1]	3 lbs	20	2
POTATOES			
Potatoes, Red Bliss (2 oz. ea) [2]	Up to 20	6	1/2
Potatoes, White, cubed [2]	3 cups	6	1/2

1 *After cooking, release pressure naturally.*
2 *After cooking, release pressure manually.*
▲ *Cooking time + let rest for 1 hour on KEEP WARM*

PANTRY TIPS

Being prepared to cook the recipes in this book, or any recipe for that matter, is one of the keys to success in the kitchen. Your pantry must be stocked with the basics. We all know how frustrating it can be when you go to the cupboard and what you need is not there. This list includes some of the ingredients you will find in this book and some that are important to always have on hand.

PANTRY	REFRIGERATOR	FREEZER	ON MY COUNTER
Olive Oils	Carrots	Garlic Ginger Starter	Bananas
Canola Oils	Celery	Pesto	Onions
Kosher Salt	Garlic	Ground Beef	White Potatoes
Black Peppercorn to Grind Fresh	Ginger	Chicken	Squash
Chicken-Flavored Bouillon Powder or Base	Lemons	Vegetarian Meat Substitute	Garlic Bulbs
Beef-Flavored Bouillon Powder or Base	Limes	Any Meats on Sale/in Bulk	Tomatoes
Vegetable-Flavored Bouillon Powder or Base	Basil, Cilantro, Sage & Green Onions	Peas	
Cayenne Pepper	Dark, Leafy Greens	Broccoli	
Variety of Dried Spices	Lettuce	Raspberries	
Garlic, Fresh & Granulated	Mushrooms	Spinach	
Onion, Fresh & Granulated	Parmesan Cheese	Dark, Leafy Greens Such as Kale, Collards, Turnip Greens	
Vinegar, White, Apple Cider & Balsamic	Cabbage		
Worcestershire Sauce	Eggs		
Sriracha Hot Sauce	Butter		
Soy Sauce & Liquid Aminos	Apples & Citrus		
Honey	Milk & Almond Milk		
Variety of Sugars	Tofu		
Sweeteners Such as Stevia & Zsweet			
Ketchup			
Mustard, Dried, Yellow & Grainy			
Mayonnaise			
Variety of Pickles			
Pepperoncini			
Chipotle Chiles in Adobo Sauce			
Variety of Dry Beans			
Variety of Pasta			
Variety of Rice			
Canned Foods Such as Tomato, Tuna			
Green Chiles, Tomato Paste, Pasta Sauce, Soups			

POT ROAST

	5-QUART 3-4 SERVINGS	6-QUART 4-5 SERVINGS	8-QUART 6-7 SERVINGS	10-QUART 7-8 SERVINGS
BEEF CHUCK ROAST	2 POUNDS	2 1/2 POUNDS	4 POUNDS	5 POUNDS
BEEF STOCK	2 1/2 CUPS	3 CUPS	5 CUPS	6 CUPS
KOSHER SALT AND FRESH PEPPER	TO TASTE	TO TASTE	TO TASTE	TO TASTE
ALL PURPOSE FLOUR OR CORNSTARCH	1 TBSP	2 TBSP	3 TBSP	4 TBSP
SOY SAUCE, BOTTLED	2 TBSP	3 TBSP	4 TBSP	5 TBSP
RED POTATOES, SMALL	8	10	16	18
CARROTS, CHUNKED	2	3	4	5
PEARL ONIONS, FROZEN (10 OZ SIZE BAG)	1 BAG	1 BAG	2 BAGS	2 BAGS
CELERY, CHUNKED	1	2	2	3
BAY LEAF	1	1	2	2
KETCHUP	1/4 CUP	1/3 CUP	1/2 CUP	2/3 CUP

Method:

1. *Place all ingredients into the pressure cooker; stir well then secure lid.*
2. *Set steam vent to SEAL and timer to 40 minutes.*
3. *When cooking is complete, let pressure release naturally.*
4. *Remove, garnish as desired and serve.*

TIP

This is an excellent dish to keep in the freezer so you always have a delicious dinner ready when in a pinch.

MAC & CHEESE

	5-QUART 3-4 SERVINGS	6-QUART 4-5 SERVINGS	8-QUART 5-6 SERVINGS	10-QUART 6-7 SERVINGS
PASTA, SMALL SIZE, DRY	1 1/2 CUPS	1 3/4 CUPS	2 1/4 CUPS	3 CUPS
CHICKEN OR VEGETABLE STOCK	2 1/2 CUPS	2 3/4 CUPS	3 1/2 CUPS	5 CUPS
KOSHER SALT AND FRESH PEPPER	TO TASTE	TO TASTE	TO TASTE	TO TASTE
WHOLE MILK	1 CUP	1 1/4 CUPS	1 1/2 CUPS	2 CUPS
CHEDDAR CHEESE, SHREDDED	1 CUP	1 1/4 CUPS	1 1/2 CUPS	2 CUPS
PARMESAN CHEESE, GRATED	1/2 CUP	2/3 CUP	3/4 CUPS	1 CUP
MOZZARELLA CHEESE, SHREDDED	1 1/2 CUPS	1 2/3 CUPS	2 CUPS	3 CUPS

Method:

1. *Place the pasta, stock, salt and pepper into the pressure cooker; secure lid.*
2. *Set steam vent to SEAL and timer to 6 minutes.*
3. *When cooking is complete, let pressure release naturally.*
4. *Add remaining ingredients and stir until cheeses are well melted.*
5. *Garnish as desired and serve.*

TIP

If you want a brown crust to form on the bottom, cover with lid after stirring in the cheeses (do not secure lid) then turn on the timer so the pressure cooker heats up (without pressure) which will brown the bottom in a few minutes.

WOLF'S
REISFLEISCH

	5-QUART 3-4 SERVINGS	6-QUART 4-5 SERVINGS	8-QUART 5-6 SERVINGS	10-QUART 7-8 SERVINGS
LONG-GRAIN WHITE RICE SUCH AS BASMATI, UNCOOKED	1 CUP	1 1/4 CUPS	1 1/2 CUPS	2 CUPS
KIELBASA SAUSAGE, SLICED	2 CUPS	2 1/2 CUPS	3 CUPS	4 CUPS
YELLOW ONIONS, CHOPPED	1 CUP	1 CUP	1 1/2 CUPS	2 CUPS
CARROTS, CHOPPED	1 CUP	1 CUP	1 1/2 CUPS	2 CUPS
CELERY, CHOPPED	1 CUP	1 CUP	1 1/2 CUPS	2 CUPS
BELL PEPPERS, CHOPPED	1 CUP	1 CUP	1 1/2 CUPS	2 CUPS
GARLIC CLOVES, CHOPPED	2 TBSP	2 TBSP	3 TBSP	1/4 CUP
CHILI FLAKES	TO TASTE	TO TASTE	TO TASTE	TO TASTE
PAPRIKA	1 TBSP	1 TBSP	1 1/2 TBSP	2 TBSP
TURMERIC POWDER	1 tsp	1 tsp	1 1/2 tsp	2 tsp
KOSHER SALT AND FRESH PEPPER	TO TASTE	TO TASTE	TO TASTE	TO TASTE
BUTTER, UNSALTED	2 TBSP	2 TBSP	3 TBSP	1/4 CUP
CHICKEN STOCK	1 CUP	1 1/4 CUPS	1 1/2 CUPS	2 CUPS

Method:

1. *Place all ingredients into the pressure cooker; stir well then secure lid.*
2. *Set steam vent to SEAL and timer to 6 minutes.*
3. *When cooking is complete, let pressure release naturally.*
4. *Remove, garnish as desired and serve.*

ONE POT
BEEF BOLOGNESE

	5-QUART 3-4 SERVINGS	6-QUART 4-5 SERVINGS	8-QUART 5-6 SERVINGS	10-QUART 7-8 SERVINGS
GROUND BEEF PATTIES, FRESH OR FROZEN	1 POUND	1 1/4 POUNDS	1 1/2 POUNDS	2 POUNDS
BUTTER, UNSALTED	1 TBSP	1 TBSP	1 1/2 TBSP	2 TBSP
YELLOW ONION, MEDIUM, CHOPPED	1/2 CUP	2/3 CUP	3/4 CUP	1 CUP
CELERY, CHOPPED	1/2 CUP	2/3 CUP	3/4 CUP	1 CUP
CARROTS, CHOPPED	1/2 CUP	2/3 CUP	3/4 CUP	1 CUP
GARLIC CLOVES, CHOPPED	4	4	6	8
PASTA, DRY	1 CUP	1 1/4 CUPS	1 1/2 CUPS	2 CUPS
BEEF STOCK	1 CUP	1 1/4 CUPS	1 1/2 CUPS	2 CUPS
PASTA SAUCE, JARRED	1 1/2 CUPS	1 1/2 CUPS	2 1/4 CUPS	3 CUPS
HEAVY CREAM	2 TBSP	2 TBSP	3 TBSP	1/4 CUP
KOSHER SALT AND FRESH PEPPER	TO TASTE	TO TASTE	TO TASTE	TO TASTE
CHILI FLAKES	TO TASTE	TO TASTE	TO TASTE	TO TASTE
BRANCH OF ROSEMARY	1	1	2	2
PARMESAN CHEESE, GRATED, FOR SERVING	AS DESIRED	AS DESIRED	AS DESIRED	AS DESIRED
WHOLE MILK RICOTTA CHEESE, FOR SERVING	AS DESIRED	AS DESIRED	AS DESIRED	AS DESIRED

Method:

1. *Place all ingredients, except cheeses, into the pressure cooker; secure lid.*
2. *Set steam vent to SEAL and timer to 6 minutes.*
3. *When cooking is complete, let pressure release naturally.*
4. *Stir to break up the meat if needed.*
5. *Remove, garnish as desired then serve with Parmesan cheese and ricotta.*

TIP
You can substitute ground chicken or turkey for the beef.

15

CHICKEN & MATZO BALL SOUP

	5-QUART 4-5 SERVINGS	6-QUART 5-6 SERVINGS	8-QUART 7-8 SERVINGS	10-QUART 9-10 SERVINGS
SOUP				
WHOLE CHICKEN, CUT INTO PIECES	1	1 1/4	1 + 2 BREASTS	2
CARROTS, SLICED	4	5	6	8
CELERY STALK, SLICED	1	1	1 1/2	2
YELLOW ONION, LARGE, SLICED	1	1 1/4	1 1/2	2
KOSHER SALT AND FRESH PEPPER	TO TASTE	TO TASTE	TO TASTE	TO TASTE
CHICKEN STOCK	6 CUPS	7 CUPS	9 CUPS	12 CUPS
MATZO BALLS				
LARGE EGGS	5	5	8	8
KOSHER SALT	2 tsp	2 tsp	1 TBSP	1 TBSP
ONION POWDER	1 TBSP	1 TBSP	1 1/2 TBSP	1 1/2 TBSP
CHICKEN FAT, FROM SURFACE OF SOUP	1/4 CUP	1/4 CUP	1/3 CUP	1/3 CUP
CLUB SODA	3 TBSP	3 TBSP	1/4 CUP	1/4 CUP
DILL, CHOPPED + MORE FOR SERVING	1 TBSP	1 TBSP	1 1/2 TBSP	1 1/2 TBSP
MATZO MEAL	1 CUP	1 CUP	1 1/2 CUPS	1 1/2 CUPS

Method:

1. Place all soup ingredients into the pressure cooker; secure lid.
2. Set steam vent to SEAL and timer to 30 minutes.
3. When cooking is complete, let pressure release naturally.
4. Remove lid then skim chicken fat per the table above from the soup into a mixing bowl.
5. Add remaining matzo ball ingredients to the mixing bowl and stir to combine; let stand for 10 minutes.
6. With the lid off, set timer to 20 minutes to turn on the pressure cooker.
7. When soup begins to simmer, use a small ice cream scoop or teaspoon to drop 1" balls of matzo ball mixture into the soup.
8. Cover with lid but do not SEAL; let simmer for 10 minutes.
9. Remove, garnish as desired and serve hot.

TIP

Scooping the matzo ball
mixture instead of rolling
it into balls makes for
more tender matzo balls.

SHREDDED BEEF
TACOS

	5-QUART 3-4 SERVINGS	6-QUART 4-5 SERVINGS	8-QUART 5-6 SERVINGS	10-QUART 7-8 SERVINGS
FLANK STEAK	2 POUNDS	2 1/2 POUNDS	3 1/4 POUNDS	4 POUNDS
OLIVE OIL	2 TBSP	2 1/2 TBSP	3 TBSP	1/4 CUP
CHILI POWDER, SUCH AS ANCHO (OR USE TO TASTE)	2 TBSP	2 1/2 TBSP	3 TBSP	1/4 CUP
GROUND CUMIN	2 tsp	2 1/2 tsp	3 tsp	4 tsp
GROUND CORIANDER	2 tsp	2 1/2 tsp	3 tsp	4 tsp
KOSHER SALT	TO TASTE	TO TASTE	TO TASTE	TO TASTE
BEEF STOCK	2 CUPS	2 1/2 CUPS	3 1/4 CUPS	4 CUPS
WHITE ONION, LARGE, SLICED	2	2 1/2	3 1/4	4
TACO FIXINGS OF YOUR CHOICE	AS DESIRED	AS DESIRED	AS DESIRED	AS DESIRED

Method:

1. *Place all ingredients, except taco fixings, into the pressure cooker; secure lid.*
2. *Set steam vent to SEAL and timer to 35 minutes.*
3. *When cooking is complete, let pressure release naturally.*
4. *Shred beef using tongs or 2 forks.*
5. *Remove, garnish as desired and serve with desired taco fixings.*

BUTTERNUT SQUASH SOUP

	5-QUART 3-4 SERVINGS	6-QUART 4-5 SERVINGS	8-QUART 6-7 SERVINGS	10-QUART 7-8 SERVINGS
BUTTERNUT SQUASH, CUBED	5 CUPS	6 CUPS	8 CUPS	10 CUPS
VEGETABLE STOCK (+ MORE IF NEEDED)	4 CUPS	5 CUPS	6 1/2 CUPS	8 CUPS
FRESH GINGER	1 TBSP	1 1/4 TBSP	1 3/4 TBSP	2 TBSP
HONEY	2 TBSP	2 1/2 TBSP	3 TBSP	1/4 CUP
GROUND CINNAMON	1/2 tsp	1/2 tsp	3/4 tsp	1 tsp
LEMON JUICE	1 TBSP	1 1/4 TBSP	1 1/2 TBSP	2 TBSP
KOSHER SALT AND FRESH PEPPER	TO TASTE	TO TASTE	TO TASTE	TO TASTE
CRANBERRY SAUCE, JARRED	TO TASTE	TO TASTE	TO TASTE	TO TASTE
SOUR CREAM	TO TASTE	TO TASTE	TO TASTE	TO TASTE
CHIVES, CHOPPED	TO TASTE	TO TASTE	TO TASTE	TO TASTE

Method:

1. Place the squash, stock, ginger, honey, cinnamon, lemon juice, salt and pepper into the pressure cooker; secure lid.
2. Set steam vent to SEAL and timer to 6 minutes.
3. When cooking is complete, let pressure release naturally.
4. Puree soup using an immersion blender or blender until smooth.
5. Top with cranberry sauce, sour cream and chives before serving.

TIP

Some butternut squash have more starch than others so you might need a little more stock to achieve your desired consistency.

CAROLINA
PULLED PORK

	5-QUART 2-3 SERVINGS	6-QUART 3-4 SERVINGS	8-QUART 5-6 SERVINGS	10-QUART 6-7 SERVINGS
PORK SHOULDER	2 1/2 POUNDS	3 POUNDS	5 POUNDS	6 POUNDS
DRY BBQ RUB	2 TBSP	3 TBSP	1/4 CUP	1/3 CUP
KOSHER SALT AND FRESH PEPPER	TO TASTE	TO TASTE	TO TASTE	TO TASTE
CHILI FLAKES	TO TASTE	TO TASTE	TO TASTE	TO TASTE
APPLE CIDER VINEGAR	2 TBSP	3 TBSP	1/4 CUP	1/3 CUP
YELLOW MUSTARD	2 TBSP	3 TBSP	1/4 CUP	1/3 CUP
PORK OR CHICKEN STOCK	2 CUPS	2 1/2 CUPS	3 CUPS	3 1/2 CUPS
MUSTARD-BASED BBQ SAUCE, FOR SERVING	AS DESIRED	AS DESIRED	AS DESIRED	AS DESIRED

Method:

1. *Place all ingredients, except BBQ sauce, into the pressure cooker; secure lid.*
2. *Set steam vent to SEAL and timer to 40 minutes.*
3. *When cooking is complete, let pressure release naturally.*
4. *Add BBQ sauce to the pressure cooker, stir then pull meat apart using tongs or 2 forks before serving.*

EASY FLAN

	5-QUART MAKES 1 FLAN	6-QUART MAKES 1 FLAN	8-QUART MAKES 1 FLAN	10-QUART MAKES 1 FLAN
MICROWAVE CARAMEL (SEE PAGE 88)	SEE STEP 1	SEE STEP 1	SEE STEP 1	SEE STEP 1
EVAPORATED MILK	1 CUP	1 CUP	1 CUP	1 CUP
CONDENSED MILK	1 CUP	1 CUP	1 CUP	1 CUP
LARGE EGGS	3	3	3	3
EGG YOLKS	6	6	6	6
VANILLA EXTRACT	1 tsp	1 tsp	1 tsp	1 tsp

Method:

1. *Prepare Microwave Caramel on page 88 then line a 6" cake pan with the caramel; set aside.*
2. *Using a blender or immersion blender, incorporate the milks, eggs and vanilla until completely smooth then strain mixture and pour into caramel-lined pan (you may have extra depending on the height of your cake pan). Cover top of pan with aluminum foil.*
3. *Place the steaming rack or a folded kitchen towel into the bottom of the pressure cooker.*
4. *Make a foil sling for the cake pan (see page 8).*
5. *Pour 2 cups of water into the pressure cooker then lower the cake pan into the pressure cooker using the foil sling; secure lid.*
6. *Set steam vent to SEAL and timer to 12 minutes.*
7. *When cooking is complete, carefully release the pressure manually (see tips on page 7) then remove lid.*
8. *Remove pan by the foil sling then chill flan for a minimum of 2 hours or up to 5 days.*
9. *To serve, run a thin knife around the edge of flan and invert onto a rimmed serving plate. The now liquid caramel will flow around and over it.*
10. *Garnish as desired and serve.*

RECIPES

CHOCOLATE TRUFFLE CAKE

	5-QUART MAKES 1 CAKE	6-QUART MAKES 1 CAKE	8-QUART MAKES 1 CAKE	10-QUART MAKES 1 CAKE
BITTERSWEET CHOCOLATE PIECES	5 OZ	5 OZ	5 OZ	5 OZ
BUTTER, UNSALTED	5 OZ	5 OZ	5 OZ	5 OZ
WHOLE LARGE EGGS	3	3	3	3
LARGE EGG YOLKS	3	3	3	3
GRANULATED SUGAR	1/2 CUP	1/2 CUP	1/2 CUP	1/2 CUP
ALL PURPOSE FLOUR, SIFTED	2/3 CUP	2/3 CUP	2/3 CUP	2/3 CUP
CHOCOLATE ICING, STORE-BOUGHT	AS DESIRED	AS DESIRED	AS DESIRED	AS DESIRED
CHOCOLATE SAUCE	AS DESIRED	AS DESIRED	AS DESIRED	AS DESIRED
WALNUTS, TOASTED AND CHOPPED	AS DESIRED	AS DESIRED	AS DESIRED	AS DESIRED

Method:

1. *Apply nonstick cooking spray to a 6" cake pan then line the bottom with parchment paper or aluminum foil; set aside.*
2. *In a microwave-safe bowl, combine the chocolate and butter; heat until melted.*
3. *Using a hand mixer and a medium bowl, beat the eggs, egg yolks and sugar for 5 minutes or until pale and fluffy.*
4. *Stir in the chocolate mixture and flour until smooth then pour into prepared pan.*
5. *Place the steaming rack or a folded kitchen towel into the bottom of the pressure cooker.*
6. *Make a foil sling for the cake pan (see page 8).*
7. *Pour 2 cups of water into the pressure cooker then lower the cake pan into the pressure cooker using the foil sling; secure lid.*
8. *Set steam vent to SEAL and timer to 20 minutes.*
9. *When cooking is complete, carefully release the pressure manually (see tips on page 7) then remove lid.*
10. *Remove pan by the foil sling then let cool for 30 minutes.*
11. *Frost with icing, drizzle with chocolate sauce and sprinkle with walnuts before serving.*

TIP

To toast the walnuts, place them on a sheet pan and bake for 10-12 minutes at 350°F or until browned and fragrant. You can also frost the top of this cake with creamy peanut putter and sprinkle with peanuts as an alternative.

CORNED BEEF & CABBAGE

	5-QUART 3-4 SERVINGS	6-QUART 4-5 SERVINGS	8-QUART 5-6 SERVINGS	10-QUART 7-8 SERVINGS
CORNED BEEF, TRIMMED	2-3 POUNDS	3-4 POUNDS	4-5 POUNDS	5-6 POUNDS
PICKLING SPICE (OPTIONAL)	1 TBSP	1 1/4 TBSP	1 1/2 TBSP	2 TBSP
CARROTS, CHUNKED	3	4	5	6
YELLOW ONION, MEDIUM, CHUNKED	1	1 1/4	1 3/4	2
RED POTATOES, SMALL	6	8	10	12
GREEN CABBAGE WEDGES	3	4	5	6
BEER OR WATER	3 CUPS	4 CUPS	5 CUPS	6 CUPS
PARSLEY, CHOPPED, FOR SERVING	AS DESIRED	AS DESIRED	AS DESIRED	AS DESIRED

Method:

1. *Place all ingredients, except parsley, into the pressure cooker; secure lid.*
2. *Set steam vent to SEAL and timer to 90 minutes.*
3. *When cooking is complete, let pressure release naturally.*
4. *Top with parsley, garnish as desired and serve.*

TIP

If you prefer firmer vegetables, add them to the pressure cooker towards the end of cooking. Manually release the pressure (see tips on page 7) with 6 minutes of cooking time remaining, add to pressure cooker, secure lid then let cook for the remaining 6 minutes.

PLAIN WHITE RICE

	5-QUART 3-4 SERVINGS	6-QUART 4-5 SERVINGS	8-QUART 5-6 SERVINGS	10-QUART 6-7 SERVINGS
PLAIN WHITE RICE, SUCH AS BASMATI, UNCOOKED	1 CUP	2 CUPS	3 CUPS	4 CUPS
WATER	1 CUP	2 CUPS	3 CUPS	4 CUPS
KOSHER SALT (OPTIONAL)	TO TASTE	TO TASTE	TO TASTE	TO TASTE

Method:

1. *Place all ingredients into the pressure cooker; secure lid.*
2. *Set steam vent to SEAL and timer to 6 minutes.*
3. *When cooking is complete, let pressure release naturally.*
4. *Let rice stand on KEEP WARM for 10 minutes or more if needed until all the way tender.*
5. *Remove, garnish as desired and serve.*

CURRY IN A HURRY

	5-QUART 4-5 SERVINGS	6-QUART 5-6 SERVINGS	8-QUART 6-7 SERVINGS	10-QUART 7-8 SERVINGS
DESIRED CHICKEN PIECES (CAN BE FROZEN)	2 POUNDS	2 1/2 POUNDS	3 POUNDS	4 POUNDS
COCONUT OR VEGETABLE OIL	2 TBSP	2 TBSP	3 TBSP	1/4 CUP
KOSHER SALT AND FRESH PEPPER	TO TASTE	TO TASTE	TO TASTE	TO TASTE
YELLOW ONION, LARGE, CHOPPED	1	1 1/4	1 3/4	2
GARLIC CLOVES, CHOPPED	4	5	6	8
FRESH GINGER, CHOPPED	1 TBSP	1 TBSP	2 TBSP	2 TBSP
CHILI FLAKES	TO TASTE	TO TASTE	TO TASTE	TO TASTE
COCONUT MILK	2 CUPS	2 1/2 CUPS	3 CUPS	4 CUPS
CHICKEN STOCK	1 CUP	1 1/4 CUPS	1 3/4 CUPS	2 CUPS
CURRY POWDER	2 TBSP	2 TBSP	3 TBSP	3 TBSP
FRESH LIME JUICE	1 TBSP	1 1/4 TBSP	1 3/4 TBSP	2 TBSP
HONEY	1 TBSP	1 1/4 TBSP	1 3/4 TBSP	2 TBSP
CORNSTARCH	2 TBSP	2 1/4 TBSP	3 TBSP	4 TBSP
TOMATO JUICE	1/3 CUP	1/3 CUP	1/2 CUP	2/3 CUP
CILANTRO + MORE FOR SERVING	1 TBSP	1 1/4 TBSP	1 3/4 TBSP	2 TBSP
BROWN RICE, FOR SERVING (SEE PAGE 58)	AS DESIRED	AS DESIRED	AS DESIRED	AS DESIRED

Method:

1. *Place all ingredients, except cornstarch, tomato juice, cilantro and rice, into the pressure cooker; secure lid.*
2. *Set steam vent to SEAL and timer to 9 minutes.*
3. *When cooking is complete, let pressure release naturally.*
4. *Remove lid then set timer to 5 minutes to turn cooker back on to boil contents (keep uncovered, do not secure lid).*
5. *Stir cornstarch into tomato juice until smooth then stir into bubbling pressure cooker contents.*
6. *Stir constantly for 2 minutes or until thickened and smooth.*
7. *Garnish with cilantro then serve as desired over brown rice.*

RECIPES

LAMB SHANKS

	5-QUART 3 SERVINGS	6-QUART 4 SERVINGS	8-QUART 5 SERVINGS	10-QUART 6 SERVINGS
LAMB SHANKS, MEDIUM SIZE	3	4	5	6
PAPRIKA	2 TBSP	3 TBSP	1/4 CUP	1/3 CUP
KOSHER SALT AND FRESH PEPPER	TO TASTE	TO TASTE	TO TASTE	TO TASTE
BEEF STOCK	1 1/2 CUPS	2 CUPS	3 CUPS	4 CUPS
PASTA SAUCE, JARRED	2 CUPS	2 CUPS	3 CUPS	3 CUPS
PEARL ONIONS, FROZEN (10 OZ SIZE BAG)	1 BAG	1 BAG	1 BAG	1 BAG
MIXED OLIVES	3/4 CUP	1 CUP	1 1/2 CUPS	2 CUPS
FRESH ROSEMARY	1 1/2 SPRIGS	2 SPRIGS	2 1/2 SPRIGS	3 SPRIGS
GARLIC CLOVES, WHOLE	1/3 CUP	1/2 CUP	2/3 CUP	2/3 CUP
OLIVE OIL	2 TBSP	3 TBSP	1/4 CUP	1/3 CUP

Method:

1. Rub each lamb shank thoroughly with paprika, salt and pepper then transfer to the pressure cooker.
2. Add remaining ingredients to the pressure cooker; secure lid.
3. Set steam vent to SEAL and timer to 35 minutes.
4. When cooking is complete, let pressure release naturally.
5. Garnish as desired and serve.

TIP

These lamb shanks are best served over the mashed potatoes on page 34.

EASY
LASAGNA

	5-QUART 3-4 SERVINGS	6-QUART 4-5 SERVINGS	8-QUART 5-6 SERVINGS	10-QUART 6-7 SERVINGS
ITALIAN SAUSAGE, CRUMBLED	1 POUND	1 1/4 POUNDS	1 3/4 POUNDS	2 POUNDS
YELLOW ONION, MEDIUM, CHOPPED	1	1 1/4	1 3/4	2
GARLIC CLOVES, CHOPPED	4	5	6	8
PASTA SAUCE, JARRED	2 CUPS	2 1/2 CUPS	3 CUPS	4 CUPS
BEEF STOCK	2 CUPS	2 1/2 CUPS	3 CUPS	4 CUPS
KOSHER SALT AND FRESH PEPPER	TO TASTE	TO TASTE	TO TASTE	TO TASTE
LASAGNA NOODLES, DRY (BROKEN INTO 2" PIECES)	8 NOODLES	10 NOODLES	12 NOODLES	16 NOODLES
PARMESAN CHEESE, GRATED	1/2 CUP	2/3 CUP	3/4 CUP	1 CUP
MOZZARELLA CHEESE, SHREDDED	1 1/2 CUPS	2 CUPS	2 1/2 CUPS	3 CUPS
WHOLE MILK RICOTTA CHEESE	1/2 CUP	2/3 CUP	3/4 CUP	1 CUP

Method:

1. *Place all ingredients, except cheeses, into the pressure cooker; stir well then secure lid.*
2. *Set steam vent to SEAL and timer to 6 minutes.*
3. *When cooking is complete, let pressure release naturally.*
4. *Remove lid then top with Parmesan and mozzarella cheeses but do not stir; cover with lid but don't secure it and let stand for 5-10 minutes or until cheeses are melted.*
5. *Top with dollops of ricotta cheese, garnish as desired and serve.*

RECIPES

29

BBQ
RIBS

	5-QUART 2-3 SERVINGS	6-QUART 3-4 SERVINGS	8-QUART 4-5 SERVINGS	10-QUART 5-6 SERVINGS
SLAB OF RIBS, ST. LOUIS STYLE	1	2	3	4
DRY BBQ RUB, JARRED	TO TASTE	TO TASTE	TO TASTE	TO TASTE
CHICKEN STOCK	1/2 CUP	1/2 CUP	1/2 CUP	1/2 CUP
BEER OR WATER	12 OZ	12 OZ	12 OZ	12 OZ
BBQ SAUCE, BOTTLED + MORE FOR SERVING	1 CUP	1 1/4 CUPS	1 1/2 CUPS	2 CUPS
FRESH PEPPER	TO TASTE	TO TASTE	TO TASTE	TO TASTE

RECIPES

Method:

1. *Sprinkle ribs with BBQ rub then place into the pressure cooker.*
2. *Add remaining ingredients then secure lid.*
3. *Set steam vent to SEAL and timer to 25 minutes.*
4. *When cooking is complete, let pressure release naturally.*
5. *Remove, garnish as desired and serve with additional BBQ sauce.*

TIP

For crispy edge ribs, place the cooked ribs on a foil-lined sheet pan then broil in the oven for 1-2 minutes or until desired texture is achieved.

SOUTHERN GREENS

	5-QUART 4-5 SERVINGS	6-QUART 4-5 SERVINGS	8-QUART 6-7 SERVINGS	10-QUART 6-7 SERVINGS
DARK LEAFY GREENS, SUCH AS COLLARD, TURNIP OR MUSTARD	1 BUNDLE	1 BUNDLE	2 BUNDLES	2 BUNDLES
HAM HOCK OR SMOKED TURKEY WING	2	2	3	3
CHICKEN STOCK	5 CUPS	5 CUPS	10 CUPS	10 CUPS
CHILI FLAKES	TO TASTE	TO TASTE	TO TASTE	TO TASTE
APPLE CIDER VINEGAR	1 TBSP	1 TBSP	2 TBSP	2 TBSP
KOSHER SALT AND FRESH PEPPER	TO TASTE	TO TASTE	TO TASTE	TO TASTE

Method:

1. *Wash, de-stem greens then wash again. Cut greens into pieces if desired then set aside.*
2. *Place remaining ingredients into the pressure cooker then set timer to 9 minutes with the lid off. When broth is boiling, add a large handful of the greens and push them down using a spoon.*
3. *As soon as they are wilted, repeat with another handful and continue until all greens are wilted down and below the MAX line (this process only takes a few minutes); secure lid.*
4. *Set steam vent to SEAL and timer to 9 minutes.*
5. *When cooking is complete, let pressure release naturally.*
6. *Remove, garnish as desired and serve.*

TIP
If you like your greens a bit firmer, change cooking time to 3 minutes.

STEEL CUT

OATMEAL

	5-QUART 3-4 SERVINGS	6-QUART 4-5 SERVINGS	8-QUART 5-6 SERVINGS	10-QUART 6-7 SERVINGS
STEEL CUT OATS	1 CUP	1 1/4 CUPS	1 1/2 CUPS	2 CUPS
WATER	4 CUPS	5 CUPS	6 CUPS	8 CUPS
KOSHER SALT (OPTIONAL)	TO TASTE	TO TASTE	TO TASTE	TO TASTE
BERRIES OR OTHER DESIRED TOPPINGS	AS DESIRED	AS DESIRED	AS DESIRED	AS DESIRED

Method:

1. *Place all ingredients, except berries or other toppings, into the pressure cooker; secure lid.*
2. *Set steam vent to SEAL and timer to 9 minutes.*
3. *When cooking is complete, let pressure release naturally.*
4. *Oats will appear quite runny at first but will thicken as you stir.*
5. *Remove, garnish as desired and serve.*

TIP

it is important to let
the pressure release
naturally to avoid
any hot liquid from
bubbling out of the
steam vent.

MASHED

POTATOES

	5-QUART 4 SERVINGS	6-QUART 5 SERVINGS	8-QUART 6 SERVINGS	10-QUART 7 SERVINGS
YUKON GOLD POTATOES, PEELED AND CHUNKED	3 POUNDS	4 POUNDS	5 POUNDS	6 POUNDS
WATER	1/3 CUP	1/3 CUP	1/3 CUP	1/3 CUP
KOSHER SALT	TO TASTE	TO TASTE	TO TASTE	TO TASTE
BUTTER + MORE FOR SERVING	AS DESIRED	AS DESIRED	AS DESIRED	AS DESIRED
HEAVY CREAM, HALF & HALF OR MILK	AS NEEDED	AS NEEDED	AS NEEDED	AS NEEDED

Method:

1. *Place the potatoes, water and salt into the pressure cooker; secure lid.*
2. *Set steam vent to SEAL and timer to 6 minutes.*
3. *When cooking is complete, let pressure release naturally.*
4. *Pour off the small amount of water from the potatoes.*
5. *Use a potato masher to mash potatoes inside pressure cooker or use a potato ricer for smoother, lump-free mashed potatoes.*
6. *Add butter as well as cream and mash until desired texture is achieved.*
7. *Set pressure cooker to KEEP WARM to allow potatoes to stay hot until ready to serve.*
8. *Top with additional melted butter if desired before serving.*

TIP

The KEEP WARM feature of your pressure cooker is perfect for entertaining to keep side dishes such as mashed potatoes piping hot. You can even use it as a buffet warmer.

6-MINUTE FETTUCCINI ALFREDO

	5-QUART 3-4 SERVINGS	6-QUART 4-5 SERVINGS	8-QUART 5-6 SERVINGS	10-QUART 6-8 SERVINGS
CHICKEN TENDERS, RAW (CAN BE FROZEN)	8	10	12	16
FETTUCCINI NOODLES, DRY	8 OZ	10 OZ	12 OZ	16 OZ
CHICKEN STOCK	1 1/4 CUPS	1 1/2 CUPS	2 CUPS	3 CUPS
WHITE WINE, DRY	1/4 CUP	1/3 CUP	1/2 CUP	2/3 CUP
GARLIC CLOVES, CHOPPED	2	3	4	6
HALF & HALF	1 CUP	1 1/3 CUPS	2 CUPS	3 CUPS
PARMESAN CHEESE, GRATED	1 CUP	1 1/3 CUPS	2 CUPS	3 CUPS
KOSHER SALT AND FRESH PEPPER	TO TASTE	TO TASTE	TO TASTE	TO TASTE
PARSLEY, CHOPPED	1 TBSP	1 1/2 TBSP	2 TBSP	3 TBSP

Method:

1. *Place the chicken, noodles (broken to fit cooking pot), stock and wine into the pressure cooker; secure lid.*
2. *Set steam vent to SEAL and timer to 8 minutes.*
3. *When cooking is complete, let pressure release naturally.*
4. *Stir in remaining ingredients until well combined.*
5. *Garnish as desired and serve.*

TIP

For a vegetarian alternative, omit the chicken and replace chicken stock with vegetable stock.

AMERICAN GOULASH

	5-QUART 3-4 SERVINGS	6-QUART 4-5 SERVINGS	8-QUART 5-6 SERVINGS	10-QUART 6-8 SERVINGS
GROUND BEEF (CAN BE FROZEN)	1 POUND	1 1/4 POUNDS	1 3/4 POUNDS	2 POUNDS
YELLOW ONION, LARGE, DICED	1	1	1 1/2	2
CANNED STEWED TOMATOES (14.5 OZ SIZE)	1 CAN	1 CAN	1 1/2 CANS	2 CANS
KOSHER SALT AND FRESH PEPPER	TO TASTE	TO TASTE	TO TASTE	TO TASTE
BEEF STOCK	2 CUPS	2 1/4 CUPS	3 CUPS	4 CUPS
SMALL PASTA, DRY	2 CUPS	2 1/4 CUPS	3 CUPS	4 CUPS
KETCHUP	1/4 CUP	1/4 CUP	1/3 CUP	1/2 CUP
CHEDDAR CHEESE, SHREDDED	1 CUP	1 CUP	1 1/2 CUPS	2 CUPS

Method:

1. Place all ingredients, except cheese, into the pressure cooker; secure lid.
2. Set steam vent to SEAL and timer to 6 minutes.
3. When cooking is complete, let pressure release naturally.
4. Break up the beef using a wooden spoon if desired then stir in the cheese.
5. Garnish as desired and serve or freeze up to 3 months.

BBQ CHICKEN BREAST

	5-QUART 3 SERVINGS	6-QUART 4 SERVINGS	8-QUART 6 SERVINGS	10-QUART 8 SERVINGS
CHICKEN BREASTS, (CAN BE FROZEN)	3	4	6	8
BBQ SEASONING, STORE-BOUGHT	1 TBSP	1 1/4 TBSP	1 1/2 TBSP	2 TBSP
CHICKEN STOCK	1/2 CUP	1/2 CUP	2/3 CUP	3/4 CUP
BBQ SAUCE, BOTTLED	AS DESIRED	AS DESIRED	AS DESIRED	AS DESIRED

Method:

1. *Place the chicken into the pressure cooker then sprinkle with BBQ seasoning.*
2. *Pour stock around the chicken in the pressure cooker, allowing the seasoning to stay on the chicken; secure lid.*
3. *Set steam vent to SEAL and timer to 8 minutes.*
4. *When cooking is complete, let pressure release naturally.*
5. *Pour BBQ sauce over the chicken and let stand for 5 minutes to heat sauce.*
6. *Remove, garnish as desired and serve.*

RECIPES

TIP
This chicken freezes well
for up to 3 months.

BEEF &

BROCCOLI

	5-QUART 3 SERVINGS	6-QUART 4 SERVINGS	8-QUART 5 SERVINGS	10-QUART 6 SERVINGS
YELLOW ONION, LARGE, SLICED	1	1 1/4	1 1/2	2
BELL PEPPER, SLICED	1	1 1/4	1 1/2	2
GARLIC CLOVES, CHOPPED	3	4	5	6
FRESH GINGER, CHOPPED	1 TBSP	1 TBSP	1 1/2 TBSP	2 TBSP
SOY SAUCE, BOTTLED	TO TASTE	TO TASTE	TO TASTE	TO TASTE
BEEF STOCK	1/2 CUP	2/3 CUP	3/4 CUP	1 CUP
OYSTER SAUCE, BOTTLED	1/3 CUP	1/3 CUP	1/2 CUP	2/3 CUP
HOISIN SAUCE, BOTTLED	1/4 CUP	1/4 CUP	1/3 CUP	1/2 CUP
SIRLOIN BEEF, RAW, THINLY SLICED	1 POUND	1 1/4 POUNDS	1 1/2 POUNDS	2 POUNDS
BROCCOLI FLORETS (FRESH OR FROZEN)	2 CUPS	2 1/2 CUPS	3 CUPS	4 CUPS
GREEN ONIONS, SLICED	AS DESIRED	AS DESIRED	AS DESIRED	AS DESIRED

Method:

1. *Place all ingredients, except green onions, into the pressure cooker; stir well then secure lid.*
2. *Set steam vent to SEAL and timer to 3 minutes.*
3. *When cooking is complete, carefully release the pressure manually (see tips on page 7) then remove lid.*
4. *Top with green onions, garnish as desired and serve.*

TIP
Great served with the plain white rice on page 25.

SMOTHERED PORK CHOPS

	5-QUART 4 SERVINGS	6-QUART 5 SERVINGS	8-QUART 6 SERVINGS	10-QUART 8 SERVINGS
BUTTER, UNSALTED	1 TBSP	1 1/4 TBSP	1 1/2 TBSP	2 TBSP
PORK CHOPS	4	5	6	8
YELLOW ONION, LARGE, SLICED	1	1 1/4	1 1/2	2
CARROTS, SLICED	2	2 1/2	3	4
KOSHER SALT AND FRESH PEPPER	TO TASTE	TO TASTE	TO TASTE	TO TASTE
FRESH SAGE LEAVES	3	3	3	3
CHICKEN STOCK	2 CUPS	2 1/2 CUPS	3 CUPS	4 CUPS
WHOLE MILK	1/2 CUP	2/3 CUP	3/4 CUP	1 CUP
ALL PURPOSE FLOUR OR CORNSTARCH	2 TBSP	2 1/2 TBSP	3 TBSP	1/4 CUP

Method:

1. *Place all ingredients, except stock, milk and flour, into the pressure cooker.*
2. *In a small bowl, whisk together the stock, milk and flour until smooth.*
3. *Pour over pressure cooker contents then secure lid.*
4. *Set steam vent to SEAL and timer to 25 minutes.*
5. *When cooking is complete, let pressure release naturally.*
6. *Remove, garnish as desired and serve.*

TIP

This recipe is also delicious
made with chicken breast
or thigh instead of pork.

BEEF BRISKET

	5-QUART 3-4 SERVINGS	6-QUART 4-5 SERVINGS	8-QUART 5-6 SERVINGS	10-QUART 7-8 SERVINGS
BEEF BRISKET, TRIMMED	3 POUNDS	4 POUNDS	6 POUNDS	8 POUNDS
BEEF STOCK	1 3/4 CUPS	2 CUPS	3 CUPS	4 CUPS
YELLOW ONION, LARGE, SLICED	1	1	1 1/2	2
CARROTS, SLICED	2	2	3	4
GARLIC CLOVES, SMASHED	2	3	4	6
KOSHER SALT AND FRESH PEPPER	TO TASTE	TO TASTE	TO TASTE	TO TASTE
BALSAMIC VINEGAR	2 TBSP	2 TBSP	3 TBSP	4 TBSP
SOY SAUCE, BOTTLED	2 TBSP	2 TBSP	3 TBSP	4 TBSP
BROWN SUGAR, PACKED	1 1/2 TBSP	2 TBSP	3 TBSP	4 TBSP

Method:
1. *Place all ingredients into the pressure cooker; secure lid.*
2. *Set steam vent to SEAL and timer to 90 minutes.*
3. *When cooking is complete, let pressure release naturally.*
4. *Remove then slice or shred the brisket as desired.*
5. *Serve with the vegetables and sauce.*

TIP
After removing the brisket from the pressure cooker, you can use an immersion blender to puree the vegetables and juices right inside the pressure cooker to make a lovely, thickened sauce.

BEEF CHILI

	5-QUART 3-4 SERVINGS	6-QUART 4-5 SERVINGS	8-QUART 5-6 SERVINGS	10-QUART 6-7 SERVINGS
GROUND BEEF, COARSE GRIND	1 POUND	1 1/4 POUNDS	1 3/4 POUNDS	2 POUNDS
GARLIC CLOVES, CHOPPED	3	4	6	8
YELLOW ONION, LARGE, CHOPPED	1	1 1/4	1 1/2	2
BELL PEPPER, CHOPPED	1	1 1/4	1 1/2	2
CANNED STEWED TOMATOES (14.5 OZ SIZE)	1 CAN	1 1/4 CANS	1 1/2 CANS	2 CANS
CANNED DARK RED KIDNEY BEANS (15 OZ SIZE), DRAINED	1 CAN	1 1/4 CANS	1 1/2 CANS	2 CANS
CHILI POWDER	2 TBSP	2 TBSP	3 TBSP	4 TBSP
KOSHER SALT AND FRESH PEPPER	TO TASTE	TO TASTE	TO TASTE	TO TASTE
JARRED SALSA (12 OZ SIZE)	1 JAR	1 1/4 JARS	1 1/2 JARS	2 JARS
BEEF STOCK	2 CUPS	2 1/2 CUPS	3 CUPS	4 CUPS
CORN TORTILLA CHIPS, CRUSHED	1/2 CUP	2/3 CUP	3/4 CUP	1 CUP

Method:

1. *Place all ingredients into the pressure cooker; stir well then secure lid.*
2. *Set steam vent to SEAL and timer to 30 minutes.*
3. *When cooking is complete, let pressure release naturally.*
4. *Remove, garnish as desired and serve.*

TIP

For a vegetarian alternative, omit the beef and replace the beef stock with vegetable stock.

BEER, BRATS & KRAUT

	5-QUART 3-4 SERVINGS	6-QUART 4-5 SERVINGS	8-QUART 5-6 SERVINGS	10-QUART 6-7 SERVINGS
BRATWURST-STYLE SAUSAGES, RAW	6	8	10	12
SAUERKRAUT, DRAINED	1 POUND	1 1/3 POUNDS	1 2/3 POUNDS	2 POUNDS
RED POTATOES, HALVED OR QUARTERED (DEPENDING ON SIZE)	6	8	10	12
CARROTS, CHUNKED	2	2	3	4
YELLOW ONION, SMALL, CHUNKED	1	1 1/4	1 1/2	2
BEER, SUCH AS A LAGER	12 OZ	12 OZ	24 OZ	24 OZ
PARSLEY, CHOPPED	1 TBSP	1 1/4 TBSP	1 1/2 TBSP	2 TBSP
GRAINY MUSTARD, FOR SERVING	AS NEEDED	AS NEEDED	AS NEEDED	AS NEEDED

Method:

1. *Place all ingredients, except parsley and mustard, into the pressure cooker; secure lid.*
2. *Set steam vent to SEAL and timer to 6 minutes.*
3. *When cooking is complete, carefully release the pressure manually (see tips on page 7) then remove lid.*
4. *Top with parsley, garnish as desired and serve with mustard.*

TIP
You can use water or chicken stock instead of beer.

BOURBON CHICKEN

	5-QUART 3-4 SERVINGS	6-QUART 4-5 SERVINGS	8-QUART 5-6 SERVINGS	10-QUART 6-7 SERVINGS
CHICKEN TENDERS, RAW (CAN BE FROZEN)	12	14	18	24
BOURBON	2 TBSP	2 TBSP	3 TBSP	4 TBSP
OYSTER SAUCE, BOTTLED	1/2 CUP	2/3 CUP	3/4 CUP	1 CUP
SOY SAUCE, BOTTLED	TO TASTE	TO TASTE	TO TASTE	TO TASTE
LIGHT BROWN SUGAR	1/2 CUP	1/2 CUP	2/3 CUP	3/4 CUP
GARLIC CLOVE, SMASHED	1	1	2	2
CHICKEN STOCK	1/4 CUP	1/4 CUP	1/3 CUP	1/2 CUP
SESAME SEEDS, FOR SERVING	AS DESIRED	AS DESIRED	AS DESIRED	AS DESIRED

Method:

1. *Place all ingredients, except sesame seeds, into the pressure cooker; stir well then secure lid.*
2. *Set steam vent to SEAL and timer to 8 minutes.*
3. *When cooking is complete, let pressure release naturally.*
4. *Top with sesame seeds, garnish as desired and serve over rice (see page 25) if desired.*

TIP

As an alternative, you can make this dish using boneless pork loin chops or tofu instead of chicken.

45

CHICKEN WITH
DUMPLINGS

	5-QUART 3-4 SERVINGS	6-QUART 4-5 SERVINGS	8-QUART 6-7 SERVINGS	10-QUART 7-8 SERVINGS
CHICKEN PIECES OF YOUR CHOICE	1 POUND	1 1/4 POUNDS	1 1/2 POUNDS	2 POUNDS
CANNED CREAM OF CHICKEN SOUP (11.75 OZ SIZE)	1 CAN	1 CAN	2 CANS	2 CANS
CHICKEN STOCK	2 CUPS	2 1/4 CUPS	3 CUPS	4 CUPS
WHOLE MILK	1 CUP	1 1/4 CUPS	1 1/2 CUPS	2 CUPS
KOSHER SALT AND FRESH PEPPER	TO TASTE	TO TASTE	TO TASTE	TO TASTE
YELLOW ONION, MEDIUM, CHOPPED	1	1	1 1/2	2
CARROT, CHOPPED	2	2	3	4
CELERY STALK, CHOPPED	1	1	1 1/2	2
DRY SAGE	1 tsp	1 1/4 tsp	1 1/2 tsp	2 tsp
REFRIGERATOR BISCUITS, STORE-BOUGHT (4 OZ SIZE TUBE)	1 TUBE	1 TUBE	1 1/2 TUBES	2 TUBES
PARSLEY, CHOPPED	1 TBSP	1 TBSP	1 1/2 TBSP	2 TBSP

Method:

1. *Place all ingredients, except biscuits and parsley, into the pressure cooker; secure lid.*
2. *Set steam vent to SEAL and timer to 20 minutes.*
3. *When cooking is complete, let pressure release naturally.*
4. *Remove lid then set timer to 5 minutes to turn cooker back on to boil contents (keep uncovered, do not secure lid).*
5. *Cut biscuits into 4 pieces each then roll into balls.*
6. *Roll each ball in parsley.*
7. *Carefully drop biscuits into bubbling chicken mixture inside the pressure cooker then cover with lid but do not secure lid (do not cook under pressure).*
8. *Cook dumplings for 5 minutes or until puffed and cooked through.*
9. *Garnish as desired and serve.*

TIP

For my grandchildren, I like to add some frozen peas right before serving. This helps to cool down the food to a temperature they like while sneaking in some veggies.

BROCCOLI CHEDDAR SOUP

	5-QUART 3-4 SERVINGS	6-QUART 4-5 SERVINGS	8-QUART 6-7 SERVINGS	10-QUART 7-8 SERVINGS
BROCCOLI FLORETS (FRESH OR FROZEN)	4 CUPS	5 CUPS	6 CUPS	8 CUPS
YELLOW ONION, SMALL, CHOPPED	1	1 1/4	1 1/2	2
BUTTER, UNSALTED	2 TBSP	2 1/2 TBSP	3 TBSP	4 TBSP
VEGETABLE OR CHICKEN STOCK	3 CUPS	4 CUPS	5 CUPS	6 CUPS
KOSHER SALT AND FRESH PEPPER	TO TASTE	TO TASTE	TO TASTE	TO TASTE
HOT PEPPER SAUCE, BOTTLED	TO TASTE	TO TASTE	TO TASTE	TO TASTE
HALF & HALF OR MILK	1 CUP	1 1/4 CUPS	1 1/2 CUPS	2 CUPS
CHEDDAR CHEESE, SHREDDED	1 CUP	1 1/4 CUPS	1 1/2 CUPS	2 CUPS
CROUTONS, STORE-BOUGHT	AS DESIRED	AS DESIRED	AS DESIRED	AS DESIRED

Method:

1. *Place all ingredients, except half & half, cheese and croutons, into the pressure cooker; secure lid.*
2. *Set steam vent to SEAL and timer to 6 minutes.*
3. *When cooking is complete, let pressure release naturally.*
4. *Remove lid, add half & half and cheese then stir well or puree if desired.*
5. *Top with croutons, garnish as desired and serve.*

BUFFALO CHICKEN
TENDERS

	5-QUART 3-4 SERVINGS	6-QUART 4-5 SERVINGS	8-QUART 6-7 SERVINGS	10-QUART 7-8 SERVINGS
CHICKEN TENDERS, RAW (CAN BE FROZEN)	12	14	18	24
KOSHER SALT AND FRESH PEPPER	TO TASTE	TO TASTE	TO TASTE	TO TASTE
CHICKEN STOCK	1/2 CUP	2/3 CUP	3/4 CUP	1 CUP
BUFFALO WING SAUCE, BOTTLED	2/3 CUP	3/4 CUP	1 CUP	1 1/3 CUPS
BLUE CHEESE CRUMBLES, DIVIDED	1/2 CUP	2/3 CUP	3/4 CUP	1 CUP
CELERY STICKS, FOR SERVING	AS NEEDED	AS NEEDED	AS NEEDED	AS NEEDED

Method:

1. *Place the chicken, salt, pepper, stock, wing sauce and half of the blue cheese crumbles into the pressure cooker; secure lid.*
2. *Set steam vent to SEAL and timer to 8 minutes.*
3. *When cooking is complete, let pressure release naturally.*
4. *Remove then top with remaining cheese, garnish as desired and serve with celery sticks.*

EASY CHEESECAKE

	5-QUART 4-6 SERVINGS	6-QUART 4-6 SERVINGS	8-QUART 8-10 SERVINGS	10-QUART 8-10 SERVINGS
VANILLA WAFER COOKIES	AS NEEDED	AS NEEDED	AS NEEDED	AS NEEDED
CREAM CHEESE, SOFTENED	1 POUND	1 POUND	2 POUNDS	2 POUNDS
LARGE EGGS	3	3	6	6
GRANULATED SUGAR	1/2 CUP	1/2 CUP	1 CUP	1 CUP
FRUIT TOPPING, FOR SERVING	AS DESIRED	AS DESIRED	AS DESIRED	AS DESIRED

TIP

To turn this into a chocolate cheesecake, substitute chocolate wafer cookies for the vanilla wafer cookies and add 1/3 cup cocoa powder to the batter.

Method:

1. *Apply a generous layer of nonstick cooking spray to a 6" cake pan (8" pan for larger size pressure cookers).*
2. *Press cookies, flat-side down, into the bottom of the cake pan in a single layer; set aside.*
3. *Combine the cream cheese, eggs and sugar in a food processor or blender.*
4. *Process for 10-20 seconds or until smooth then pour mixture into the cake pan over the cookie layer; cover cake pan with aluminum foil.*
5. *Place the steaming rack or a folded kitchen towel into the bottom of the pressure cooker.*
6. *Make a foil sling for the cake pan (see page 8).*
7. *Pour 2 cups of water into the pressure cooker then lower the cake pan into the pressure cooker using the foil sling; secure lid.*
8. *Set steam vent to SEAL and set timer to 20 minutes.*
9. *When cooking is complete, let pressure release naturally.*
10. *Remove pan by the foil sling then chill cheesecake for a minimum of 3 hours or up to 2 days before serving.*
11. *Serve with fruit topping.*

BEEF STEW

	5-QUART 3-4 SERVINGS	6-QUART 4-5 SERVINGS	8-QUART 6-7 SERVINGS	10-QUART 8-10 SERVINGS
STEWING BEEF, RAW	1 POUND	1 1/4 POUNDS	1 1/2 POUNDS	2 POUNDS
BEEF STOCK	2 CUPS	2 1/2 CUPS	3 CUPS	4 CUPS
RED POTATOES, SMALL	5	6	8	10
CARROTS, CHUNKED	2	2 1/2	3	4
CELERY, CHUNKED	2	2 1/2	3	4
YELLOW ONION, LARGE, CHUNKED	1	1 1/4	1 1/2	2
GARLIC CLOVES, CHOPPED	3	4	5	6
BAY LEAVES	1	1	2	2
KETCHUP	1/4 CUP	1/4 CUP	1/3 CUP	1/2 CUP
WORCESTERSHIRE SAUCE, BOTTLED	1 TBSP	1 1/4 TBSP	1 1/2 TBSP	2 TBSP
KOSHER SALT AND FRESH PEPPER	TO TASTE	TO TASTE	TO TASTE	TO TASTE
INSTANT POTATO FLAKES	AS NEEDED	AS NEEDED	AS NEEDED	AS NEEDED

Method:

1. *Place all ingredients, except potato flakes, into the pressure cooker; secure lid.*
2. *Set steam vent to SEAL and timer to 35 minutes.*
3. *When cooking is complete, let pressure release naturally.*
4. *Begin stirring in 2 tablespoons potato flakes to thicken the sauce.*
5. *Gradually add more flakes and stir until gravy reaches desired thickness.*
6. *Remove, garnish as desired and serve.*

CHEESY CHICKEN
BROCCOLI & RICE

	5-QUART 3-4 SERVINGS	6-QUART 4-5 SERVINGS	8-QUART 5-6 SERVINGS	10-QUART 6-7 SERVINGS
CHICKEN TENDERS, RAW (CAN BE FROZEN)	4	5	6	8
BROCCOLI, FROZEN	2 CUPS	2 1/2 CUPS	3 CUPS	4 CUPS
BASMATI WHITE RICE, UNCOOKED	1 CUP	1 1/4 CUPS	1 3/4 CUPS	2
CHICKEN STOCK	1 CUP	1 1/4 CUPS	1 3/4 CUPS	2
KOSHER SALT AND FRESH PEPPER	TO TASTE	TO TASTE	TO TASTE	TO TASTE
BUTTER, UNSALTED	2 TBSP	2 1/2 TBSP	3 TBSP	1/4 CUP
YELLOW ONION, MEDIUM, CHOPPED	1	1 1/4	1 1/2	2
WHOLE MILK	1 CUP	1 1/4 CUPS	1 3/4 CUPS	2 CUPS
CREAM CHEESE, SOFTENED	4 OZ	5 OZ	6 OZ	8 OZ
ITALIAN BLEND CHEESE, SHREDDED	2 CUPS	3 CUPS	3 1/2 CUPS	4 CUPS

Method:

1. Place all ingredients, except milk and cheeses, into the pressure cooker; secure lid.
2. Set steam vent to SEAL and timer to 8 minutes.
3. When cooking is complete, let pressure release naturally.
4. Remove lid then stir in the milk and cheeses until well blended.
5. Garnish as desired and serve.

BUFFALO
MAC & CHEESE

	5-QUART 3-4 SERVINGS	6-QUART 4-5 SERVINGS	8-QUART 6-7 SERVINGS	10-QUART 7-8 SERVINGS
CHICKEN TENDERS, RAW (CAN BE FROZEN)	8	10	14	16
PASTA, DRY, SMALL SIZE	2 CUPS	2 1/2 CUPS	3 CUPS	4 CUPS
CHICKEN STOCK	2 CUPS	2 1/2 CUPS	3 CUPS	4 CUPS
BUFFALO WING SAUCE, BOTTLED	1/2 CUP	2/3 CUP	3/4 CUP	1 CUP
KOSHER SALT AND FRESH PEPPER	TO TASTE	TO TASTE	TO TASTE	TO TASTE
BLUE CHEESE CRUMBLES	1/2 CUP	2/3 CUP	3/4 CUP	1 CUP
3-CHEESE ITALIAN BLEND	2 CUPS	2 1/2 CUPS	3 CUPS	4 CUPS
CHEDDAR CRACKERS, CRUMBLED, FOR TOPPING	1/2 CUP	2/3 CUP	3/4 CUP	1 CUP

Method:

1. *Place the chicken, pasta, stock, wing sauce, salt and pepper into the pressure cooker; secure lid.*
2. *Set steam vent to SEAL and timer to 8 minutes.*
3. *When cooking is complete, let pressure release naturally.*
4. *Stir in the cheeses until melted and stringy.*
5. *Top with crumbled crackers, garnish as desired and serve.*

CHICKEN
PARMESAN

	5-QUART 3-4 SERVINGS	6-QUART 4-5 SERVINGS	8-QUART 5-6 SERVINGS	10-QUART 6-7 SERVINGS
SPAGHETTI NOODLES, DRY, BROKEN TO FIT INSIDE PRESSURE COOKER	8 OZ	10 OZ	12 OZ	1 POUND
CHICKEN STOCK	1 CUP	1 1/2 CUPS	1 3/4 CUPS	2 CUPS
ITALIAN SEASONING	1 tsp	1 tsp	2 tsp	2 tsp
KOSHER SALT AND FRESH PEPPER	TO TASTE	TO TASTE	TO TASTE	TO TASTE
GARLIC CLOVES, CHOPPED	3	4	5	6
CHICKEN TENDERS, RAW (CAN BE FROZEN)	6	8	10	12
PASTA SAUCE, JARRED	2 CUPS	2 1/2 CUPS	3 CUPS	4 CUPS
PARMESAN CHEESE, GRATED	1/3 CUP	1/3 CUP	1/2 CUP	2/3 CUP
MOZZARELLA CHEESE, SHREDDED	1 CUP	1 1/2 CUPS	1 3/4 CUPS	2 CUPS
CHILI FLAKES, FOR SERVING	AS DESIRED	AS DESIRED	AS DESIRED	AS DESIRED
PARSLEY, CHOPPED, FOR SERVING	AS DESIRED	AS DESIRED	AS DESIRED	AS DESIRED

Method:

1. *Place all ingredients, except chili flakes and parsley, in the order listed into the pressure cooker (do not stir ingredients, cheese should be on top); secure lid.*
2. *Set steam vent to SEAL and timer to 8 minutes.*
3. *When cooking is complete, let pressure release naturally.*
4. *Top with chili flakes and parsley, garnish as desired and serve.*

55

CHEESY CHEESEBURGER CASSEROLE

	5-QUART 3-4 SERVINGS	6-QUART 4-5 SERVINGS	8-QUART 5-6 SERVINGS	10-QUART 6-7 SERVINGS
GROUND BEEF (CAN BE FROZEN)	1 POUND	1 1/4 POUNDS	1 1/2 POUNDS	2 POUNDS
PASTA, DRY	1 1/2 CUPS	1 3/4 CUPS	2 CUPS	3 CUPS
BEEF STOCK	2 CUPS	2 1/4 CUPS	2 3/4 CUPS	4 CUPS
KOSHER SALT AND FRESH PEPPER	TO TASTE	TO TASTE	TO TASTE	TO TASTE
YELLOW ONION, LARGE, CHOPPED	1	1 1/4	1 1/2	2
DILL PICKLE, CHOPPED	1/4 CUP	1/4 CUP	1/3 CUP	1/2 CUP
KETCHUP	1/3 CUP	1/3 CUP	1/2 CUP	2/3 CUP
YELLOW MUSTARD	1/4 CUP	1/4 CUP	1/3 CUP	1/2 CUP
AMERICAN CHEESE SLICES	8	9	10	12
CHEDDAR CHEESE, SHREDDED	1 CUP	1 CUP	1 1/2 CUPS	2 CUPS

Method:

1. *Place all ingredients, except cheeses, into the pressure cooker; secure lid.*
2. *Set steam vent to SEAL and timer to 6 minutes.*
3. *When cooking is complete, let pressure release naturally.*
4. *Remove lid, stir in the cheeses and break up the beef if needed.*
5. *Garnish as desired and serve.*

TIP

For a creamier pasta dish, stir in 1/2 cup whole milk with the cheeses after cooking.

RECIPES

56

EASY BEEF
STROGANOFF

	5-QUART 3-4 SERVINGS	6-QUART 4-6 SERVINGS	8-QUART 6-8 SERVINGS	10-QUART 8-10 SERVINGS
STEWING BEEF CUBES, RAW	1 POUND	1 1/4 POUNDS	1 1/2 POUNDS	2 POUNDS
YELLOW ONION, LARGE, SLICED	1	1 1/4	1 1/2	2
GARLIC CLOVES, CHOPPED	2	2	3	4
BUTTER, UNSALTED	2 TBSP	2 1/2 TBSP	3 TBSP	4 TBSP
BEEF STOCK	1 1/2 CUPS	2 CUPS	2 1/2 CUPS	3 CUPS
WHITE MUSHROOMS, SLICED	2 CUPS	2 1/2 CUPS	3 CUPS	4 CUPS
WHITE WINE, DRY	1/4 CUP	1/4 CUP	1/3 CUP	1/2 CUP
KOSHER SALT AND FRESH PEPPER	TO TASTE	TO TASTE	TO TASTE	TO TASTE
SOUR CREAM	1 CUP	1 1/4 CUPS	1 1/2 CUPS	2 CUPS
EGG NOODLES, COOKED, HOT	3 CUPS	4 CUPS	5 CUPS	6 CUPS
PARSLEY, CHOPPED	AS DESIRED	AS DESIRED	AS DESIRED	AS DESIRED

Method:

1. *Set timer to 20 minutes and let pressure cooker preheat for 5 minutes with the lid off.*

2. *Add the beef, onions, garlic and butter to the pressure cooker and stir until fragrant.*

3. *Add the stock, mushrooms, wine, salt and pepper then stir to combine; secure lid.*

4. *Set steam vent to SEAL and keep timer set to 20 minutes.*

5. *When cooking is complete, let pressure release naturally.*

6. *Stir in the sour cream and noodles until well combined.*

7. *Remove, top with parsley, garnish as desired and serve.*

BROWN RICE

	5-QUART 3-4 SERVINGS	6-QUART 4-5 SERVINGS	8-QUART 6-7 SERVINGS	10-QUART 7-8 SERVINGS
BROWN BASMATI RICE, UNCOOKED	2 CUPS	2 1/2 CUPS	3 CUPS	4 CUPS
WATER	2 1/4 CUPS	2 1/2 CUPS + 1 TBSP	3 1/3 CUPS	4 1/2 CUPS
KOSHER SALT (OPTIONAL)	TO TASTE	TO TASTE	TO TASTE	TO TASTE
GREEN ONIONS (OPTIONAL)	AS DESIRED	AS DESIRED	AS DESIRED	AS DESIRED

Method:

1. *Place the rice, water and salt if desired into the pressure cooker; secure lid.*
2. *Set steam vent to SEAL and timer to 15 minutes.*
3. *When cooking is complete, let rice stand on KEEP WARM for 10 minutes or more if needed until all the way tender.*
4. *Fluff rice using a fork then serve with green onions or as desired.*

TIP

If you prefer, you can season the rice with a teaspoon each garlic powder and onion powder plus a bay leaf prior to cooking.

BROCCOLI RICE CASSEROLE

	5-QUART 3-4 SERVINGS	6-QUART 4-5 SERVINGS	8-QUART 6-7 SERVINGS	10-QUART 7-8 SERVINGS
BROCCOLI FLORETS, FROZEN	1 CUP	1 1/4 CUPS	1 1/2 CUPS	2 CUPS
YELLOW ONION, LARGE, CHOPPED	1	1 1/4	1 1/2	2
BUTTER, UNSALTED	2 TBSP	2 TBSP	3 TBSP	4 TBSP
LONG-GRAIN WHITE RICE, UNCOOKED	1 CUP	1 1/4 CUPS	1 1/2 CUPS	2 CUPS
VEGETABLE OR CHICKEN STOCK	1 1/2 CUPS	2 CUPS	2 1/2 CUPS	3 CUPS
HOT PEPPER SAUCE, BOTTLED	TO TASTE	TO TASTE	TO TASTE	TO TASTE
KOSHER SALT AND FRESH PEPPER	TO TASTE	TO TASTE	TO TASTE	TO TASTE
WHOLE MILK	1 CUP	1 1/4 CUPS	1 1/2 CUPS	2 CUPS
CHEDDAR CHEESE, SHREDDED	2 CUPS	2 1/4 CUPS	3 CUPS	4 CUPS
CHEESY CRACKERS, CRUMBLED	1 CUP	1 1/4 CUPS	1 1/2 CUPS	2 CUPS

Method:

1. *Place the broccoli, onions, butter, rice, stock, hot pepper sauce, salt and pepper into pressure cooker; secure lid.*
2. *Set steam vent to SEAL and timer to 6 minutes.*
3. *When cooking is complete, let pressure release naturally.*
4. *Remove lid then stir in the milk and cheese until melted.*
5. *Top with cracker crumbs, garnish as desired and serve.*

EASY PASTA THAT
KIDS LOVE

	5-QUART 3-4 SERVINGS	6-QUART 4-5 SERVINGS	8-QUART 6-7 SERVINGS	10-QUART 7-8 SERVINGS
PEPPERONI SLICES	1/3 CUP	1/2 CUP	2/3 CUP	1 CUP
PASTA, SMALL SIZE, DRY	1 1/2 CUPS	2 CUPS	3 CUPS	4 CUPS
PASTA SAUCE, JARRED	3/4 CUP	1 CUP	1 1/2 CUPS	2 CUPS
BEEF OR CHICKEN STOCK	1 3/4 CUPS	2 CUPS	3 CUPS	4 CUPS
ONION POWDER	1/2 TBSP	1 TBSP	1 1/2 TBSP	2 TBSP
KOSHER SALT	TO TASTE	TO TASTE	TO TASTE	TO TASTE
MOZZARELLA CHEESE, SHREDDED	3/4 CUP	1 CUP	1 1/2 CUPS	2 CUPS
PARMESAN CHEESE, GRATED	1/3 CUP	1/2 CUP	2/3 CUP	1 CUP

Method:

1. *Place all ingredients in order listed into the pressure cooker; do not stir then secure lid.*
2. *Set steam vent to SEAL and timer to 6 minutes.*
3. *When cooking is complete, carefully release the pressure manually (see tips on page 7) then remove lid.*
4. *Garnish as desired and serve.*

HOMEMADE BEEF STOCK

	5-QUART MAKES 1 1/2 QUARTS	6-QUART MAKES 1 1/2 QUARTS	8-QUART MAKES 3 QUARTS	10-QUART MAKES 3 QUARTS
OLIVE OIL	2 TBSP	2 TBSP	1/4 CUP	1/4 CUP
MEATY BEEF BONES, RAW	1 1/2 POUNDS	1 1/2 POUNDS	3 POUNDS	3 POUNDS
YELLOW ONION, LARGE, ROUGHLY CHOPPED	1	1	2	2
CARROT, ROUGHLY CHOPPED	1	1	2	2
CELERY STALK, ROUGHLY CHOPPED	1	1	2	2
PEPPERCORNS	8	8	16	16
THYME SPRIGS	2	2	4	4
UNFLAVORED GELATIN (.25 OUNCE SIZE PACKET)	1 PACKET	1 PACKET	2 PACKETS	2 PACKETS
WATER, COLD	AS NEEDED	AS NEEDED	AS NEEDED	AS NEEDED

Method:

1. Set timer to 30 minutes and let pressure cooker preheat for 5 minutes with the lid off.
2. Add the oil to the pressure cooker.
3. When oil is hot, add the bones and brown them on both sides for a total of 15 minutes.
4. Place remaining ingredients into the pressure cooker then add cold water until 1" below the MAX line; secure lid.
5. Set steam vent to SEAL and keep timer set to 30 minutes.
6. When cooking is complete, let pressure release naturally.
7. Remove lid then strain stock and discard solids.
8. Use as desired or freeze for up to 3 months.

ITALIAN QUINOA

	5-QUART 3-4 SERVINGS	6-QUART 4-5 SERVINGS	8-QUART 5-6 SERVINGS	10-QUART 6-7 SERVINGS
QUINOA, UNCOOKED	1 CUP	1 1/4 CUPS	1 3/4 CUPS	2 CUPS
VEGETABLE STOCK	1 CUP	1 1/4 CUPS	1 3/4 CUPS	2 CUPS
KOSHER SALT AND FRESH PEPPER	TO TASTE	TO TASTE	TO TASTE	TO TASTE
EXTRA-VIRGIN OLIVE OIL	2 TBSP	3 TBSP	1/4 CUP	1/3 CUP
YELLOW ONION, MEDIUM, CHOPPED	1	1 1/4	1 3/4	2
BALSAMIC VINEGAR	1 TBSP	1 1/4 TBSP	1 3/4 TBSP	2 TBSP
ROSEMARY BRANCH	1	1	2	2
PINE NUTS, TOASTED	1/4 CUP	1/3 CUP	1/2 CUP	2/3 CUP
GARLIC CLOVES, CHOPPED	4	5	6	8
SUN-DRIED TOMATOES, SLICED	1/4 CUP	1/3 CUP	1/2 CUP	2/3 CUP
PARMESAN CHEESE, GRATED	1/4 CUP	1/3 CUP	1/2 CUP	2/3 CUP
GREEN ONIONS, SLICED	1 BUNCH	1 BUNCH	2 BUNCHES	2 BUNCHES

Method:

1. *Place all ingredients, except cheese and green onions, into the pressure cooker; secure lid.*
2. *Set steam vent to SEAL and timer to 6 minutes.*
3. *When cooking is complete, let pressure release naturally.*
4. *Remove lid, add cheese and green onions then stir using a fork to combine.*
5. *Garnish as desired and serve.*

EASIEST BUTTERED NOODLES

	5-QUART 3 SERVINGS	6-QUART 4 SERVINGS	8-QUART 5 SERVINGS	10-QUART 6 SERVINGS
PASTA, SMALL SIZE, DRY	1 CUP	1 1/4 CUPS	1 1/2 CUPS	2 CUPS
BUTTER, UNSALTED	1 TBSP	1 1/4 TBSP	1 1/2 TBSP	2 TBSP
WATER	1 1/4 CUPS	1 1/2 CUPS	1 3/4 CUPS	2 1/2 CUPS
KOSHER SALT	TO TASTE	TO TASTE	TO TASTE	TO TASTE
PARSLEY, CHOPPED (OPTIONAL)	TO TASTE	TO TASTE	TO TASTE	TO TASTE

Method:

1. *Place all ingredients, except parsley, into the pressure cooker; secure lid.*
2. *Set steam vent to SEAL and timer to 6 minutes.*
3. *When cooking is complete, carefully release the pressure manually (see tips on page 7) then remove lid.*
4. *Top with parsley if desired and serve.*

CUP OF GARLIC CHICKEN

	5-QUART 3-4 SERVINGS	6-QUART 4-5 SERVINGS	8-QUART 5-6 SERVINGS	10-QUART 7-8 SERVINGS
CHICKEN PIECES (CAN BE FROZEN)	2 POUNDS	2 1/2 POUNDS	3 POUNDS	4 POUNDS
GARLIC CLOVES, WHOLE	1 CUP	1 1/4 CUPS	1 1/2 CUPS	2 CUPS
CHICKEN STOCK	2 CUPS	2 1/4 CUPS	2 3/4 CUPS	4 CUPS
FRESH ROSEMARY SPRIGS	1	1	2	2
MIXED OLIVES	1 CUP	1 1/4 CUPS	1 1/2 CUPS	2 CUPS
OLIVE OIL	3 TBSP	3 TBSP	1/4 CUP	1/4 CUP
STEWED TOMATOES, CANNED	2 CUPS	2 1/2 CUPS	3 CUPS	4 CUPS
KOSHER SALT AND FRESH PEPPER	TO TASTE	TO TASTE	TO TASTE	TO TASTE
PARMESAN CHEESE, GRATED	1/2 CUP	2/3 CUP	3/4 CUP	1 CUP

Method:

1. *Place all ingredients, except cheese, into the pressure cooker; secure lid.*
2. *Set steam vent to SEAL and timer to 20 minutes.*
3. *When cooking is complete, let pressure release naturally.*
4. *Top with Parmesan cheese, garnish as desired and serve.*

TIP

This is great served with the easiest buttered noodles on page 63.

LAZY CHICKEN & POTATOES

	5-QUART 3-4 SERVINGS	6-QUART 4-5 SERVINGS	8-QUART 6-7 SERVINGS	10-QUART 7-8 SERVINGS
BUTTER, UNSALTED	1 TBSP	1 1/2 TBSP	1 3/4 TBSP	2 TBSP
DESIRED CHICKEN PIECES (CAN BE FROZEN)	1 POUND	1 1/4 POUNDS	1 3/4 POUNDS	2 POUNDS
PAPRIKA	2 tsp	2 1/2 tsp	2 3/4 tsp	1 TBSP
RED POTATOES, SMALL	8	10	12	16
PEARL ONIONS, FROZEN (10 OZ SIZE BAG)	1 BAG	1 BAG	1 BAG	1 BAG
KOSHER SALT AND FRESH PEPPER	TO TASTE	TO TASTE	TO TASTE	TO TASTE
CAPERS	2 TBSP	2 TBSP	3 TBSP	3 TBSP
LEMON SLICES	4	5	6	8
WHITE WINE, DRY	3 TBSP	1/4 CUP	1/3 CUP	1/2 CUP
CHICKEN STOCK	1/2 CUP	2/3 CUP	3/4 CUP	1 CUP

Method:

1. *Place all ingredients into the pressure cooker; secure lid.*
2. *Set steam vent to SEAL and timer to 8 minutes.*
3. *When cooking is complete, let pressure release naturally.*
4. *Garnish as desired and serve.*

EASY
MEATLOAF

	5-QUART 4-5 SERVINGS	6-QUART 4-5 SERVINGS	8-QUART 6-8 SERVINGS	10-QUART 6-8 SERVINGS
MEATLOAF				
BREAD SLICES (SUCH AS ITALIAN BREAD)	2	2	3	3
YELLOW ONION, SMALL, CHUNKED	1/2	1/2	3/4	3/4
WHITE MUSHROOMS	8	8	12	12
UNFLAVORED GELATIN (.25 OZ SIZE PACKET)	1 PACKET	1 PACKET	1 1/2 PACKETS	1 1/2 PACKETS
LARGE EGGS	1	1	2	2
WHOLE MILK	1/2 CUP	1/2 CUP	3/4 CUP	3/4 CUP
GROUND BEEF	8 OZ	8 OZ	12 OZ	12 OZ
GROUND PORK	8 OZ	8 OZ	12 OZ	12 OZ
KOSHER SALT AND FRESH PEPPER	TO TASTE	TO TASTE	TO TASTE	TO TASTE
SOY SAUCE, BOTTLED	1 TBSP	1 TBSP	1 1/2 TBSP	1 1/2 TBSP
GLAZE				
KETCHUP	1/2 CUP	1/2 CUP	3/4 CUP	3/4 CUP
YELLOW MUSTARD	2 TBSP	2 TBSP	3 TBSP	3 TBSP
GRANULATED SUGAR	2 TBSP	2 TBSP	3 TBSP	3 TBSP

Method:

1. *Place the bread, onions, mushrooms, gelatin, egg and milk into a food processor.*
2. *Pulse until pieces are small then transfer to a large mixing bowl.*
3. *Gently fold in remaining meatloaf ingredients then pat mixture into a greased cake pan that fits inside your pressure cooker.*
4. *Stir together all glaze ingredients then spread over meatloaf in cake pan.*
5. *Place the steaming rack or a folded kitchen towel into the bottom of the pressure cooker.*
6. *Make a foil sling for the cake pan (see page 8).*
7. *Pour 2 cups of water into the pressure cooker then lower the cake pan into the pressure cooker using the foil sling; secure lid.*
8. *Set steam vent to SEAL and timer to 25 minutes.*
9. *When cooking is complete, let pressure release naturally.*
10. *Remove pan by the foil sling, garnish as desired and serve.*

TIP

Using a foil sling is a great way to help you remove the cake pan from the hot pressure cooker after cooking. See page 8 for detailed instructions on how to make and use a foil sling.

GAME DAY
SAUSAGE DIP

	5-QUART 4-6 SERVINGS	6-QUART 6-8 SERVINGS	8-QUART 8-10 SERVINGS	10-QUART 10-12 SERVINGS
BREAKFAST-STYLE SAUSAGE, BULK, CRUMBLED	3/4 POUND	1 POUND	2 POUNDS	3 POUNDS
BEEF STOCK	3/4 CUP	1 CUP	2 CUPS	2 1/2 CUPS
YELLOW ONION, LARGE, CHOPPED	1/2	1	1 1/2	2
GARLIC CLOVES, CHOPPED	2	3	4	5
WHOLE MILK	3/4 CUP	1 CUP	2 CUPS	2 1/2 CUPS
KETCHUP	1/4 CUP	1/3 CUP	2/3 CUP	3/4 CUP
KOSHER SALT AND FRESH PEPPER	TO TASTE	TO TASTE	TO TASTE	TO TASTE
CREAM CHEESE, SOFTENED	6 OZ	8 OZ	10 OZ	12 OZ
AMERICAN CHEESE SLICES	10	12	16	18
PARMESAN CHEESE, GRATED	1/3 CUP	1/2 CUP	1 CUP	1 1/4 CUPS
MOZZARELLA CHEESE, SHREDDED	1 1/2 CUPS	2 CUPS	3 CUPS	4 CUPS

Method:

1. *Place all ingredients, except cheeses, into the pressure cooker; secure lid.*
2. *Set steam vent to SEAL and timer to 9 minutes.*
3. *When cooking is complete, carefully release the pressure manually (see tips on page 7) then remove lid.*
4. *Stir in the cheeses until melted.*
5. *Let stand on KEEP WARM until ready to serve.*

TIP

You can use your pressure cooker as an informal buffet server. The KEEP WARM feature keeps the food at a steady 180°F which is perfect for serving.

CHICKEN CACCIATORE

	5-QUART 3-4 SERVINGS	6-QUART 4-5 SERVINGS	8-QUART 5-6 SERVINGS	10-QUART 6-7 SERVINGS
CHICKEN, BREASTS OR THIGHS (CAN BE FROZEN)	3	4	5	6
YELLOW ONION, LARGE, SLICED	1	1 1/2	1 3/4	2
GARLIC CLOVES, MINCED	4	5	6	8
BELL PEPPER, SLICED	1	1 1/2	1 3/4	2
STEWED TOMATOES, CANNED	2 CUPS	2 1/2 CUPS	3 CUPS	4 CUPS
OLIVE OIL	3 TBSP	3 TBSP	4 TBSP	4 TBSP
WHITE MUSHROOMS, SLICED	2 CUPS	2 1/2 CUPS	3 CUPS	4 CUPS
OREGANO, DRIED	1 tsp	1 1/2 tsp	1 3/4 tsp	2 tsp
CHICKEN STOCK	1 1/2 CUPS	2 CUPS	2 1/2 CUPS	3 CUPS
KOSHER SALT AND FRESH PEPPER	TO TASTE	TO TASTE	TO TASTE	TO TASTE
OLIVES, MIXED	1 CUP	1 1/2 CUPS	1 3/4 CUPS	2 CUPS
RED POTATOES, SMALL	6	8	10	12
PARSLEY, FOR SERVING	AS DESIRED	AS DESIRED	AS DESIRED	AS DESIRED

Method:

1. *Place all ingredients, except parsley, into the pressure cooker; secure lid.*
2. *Set steam vent to SEAL and timer to 8 minutes.*
3. *When cooking is complete, let pressure release naturally.*
4. *Remove, garnish as desired and serve.*

PEPPERONI PIZZA PASTA

	5-QUART 3-4 SERVINGS	6-QUART 4-5 SERVINGS	8-QUART 5-6 SERVINGS	10-QUART 6-7 SERVINGS
PEPPERONI SLICES	3/4 CUP	1 CUP	1 1/2 CUPS	2 CUPS
PASTA, DRY	3/4 CUP	1 CUP	1 1/2 CUPS	2 CUPS
BEEF STOCK	3/4 CUP	1 CUP	1 1/2 CUPS	2 CUPS
PASTA SAUCE, JARRED	3/4 CUP	1 CUP	1 1/2 CUPS	2 CUPS
MOZZARELLA CHEESE, SHREDDED	3/4 CUP	1 CUP	1 1/2 CUPS	2 CUPS

Method:

1. *Place all ingredients into the pressure cooker but do not stir; secure lid.*
2. *Set steam vent to SEAL and timer to 6 minutes.*
3. *When cooking is complete, let pressure release naturally.*
4. *Remove, garnish as desired and serve.*

TIP

You can add frozen veggies to this recipe before cooking to make it a complete 1-pot meal.

CHICKEN &

YELLOW RICE

RECIPES

	5-QUART 3-4 SERVINGS	6-QUART 4-5 SERVINGS	8-QUART 5-6 SERVINGS	10-QUART 6-7 SERVINGS
CHICKEN, BONELESS SKINLESS THIGHS OR BREASTS (CAN BE FROZEN)	3	4	5	6
GARLIC CLOVES, CHOPPED	4	5	6	8
RED BELL PEPPER, SLICED	1	1 1/4	1 1/2	2
TOMATO, SMALL, DICED	1	1 1/4	1 1/2	2
CHICKEN STOCK	1 CUP	1 1/2 CUPS	1 3/4 CUPS	2 CUPS
OREGANO, DRIED	1 tsp	1 1/2 tsp	1 3/4 tsp	2 tsp
OLIVE OIL	3 TBSP	1/4 CUP	1/4 CUP	1/3 CUP
GROUND TURMERIC	1 tsp	1 1/2 tsp	1 3/4 tsp	2 tsp
WHITE BASMATI RICE, UNCOOKED	1 CUP	1 1/4 CUPS	1 3/4 CUPS	2 CUPS
PEAS, FROZEN	1 CUP	1 1/2 CUPS	1 3/4 CUPS	2 CUPS

Method:

1. *Place all ingredients, except peas, into the pressure cooker; secure lid.*
2. *Set steam vent to SEAL and timer to 8 minutes.*
3. *When cooking is complete, let pressure release naturally.*
4. *Remove lid then add the peas and gently fluff the rice using a fork.*
5. *Garnish as desired and serve.*

REFRIED BEANS FROM SCRATCH

	5-QUART 3-4 SERVINGS	6-QUART 4-5 SERVINGS	8-QUART 5-6 SERVINGS	10-QUART 7-8 SERVINGS
PINTO BEANS, DRY	2 CUPS	2 1/2 CUPS	3 CUPS	4 CUPS
WHITE ONION, LARGE, CHOPPED, DIVIDED	2	2	3	4
WATER	8 CUPS	9 CUPS	12 CUPS	16 CUPS
CANOLA OIL (USE LESS IF DESIRED)	1/4 CUP	1/3 CUP	1/2 CUP	2/3 CUP
KOSHER SALT	TO TASTE	TO TASTE	TO TASTE	TO TASTE

Method:

1. Place beans, half of the onions and water into the pressure cooker; secure lid.
2. Set steam vent to SEAL and timer to 18 minutes.
3. When cooking is complete, let pressure release naturally then let stand on KEEP WARM for 1 hour.
4. Remove 2/3 of the bean liquid and reserve it.
5. Set timer to 20 minutes and keep the lid off.
6. Add remaining onions, oil and salt to the pressure cooker and let simmer for 20 minutes with the lid off while stirring often then unplug the pressure cooker.
7. Puree coarsely using an immersion blender or potato masher (add some of the reserved bean liquid if mixture is too thick).
8. Remove, garnish as desired and serve.

RICE PUDDING

	5-QUART 3-4 SERVINGS	6-QUART 3-4 SERVINGS	8-QUART 6-8 SERVINGS	10-QUART 6-8 SERVINGS
SHORT-GRAIN WHITE RICE, UNCOOKED	1 CUP	1 CUP	2 CUPS	2 CUPS
WATER	1 CUP	1 CUP	2 CUPS	2 CUPS
VANILLA EXTRACT	1 TBSP	1 TBSP	2 TBSP	2 TBSP
CINNAMON STICK	1	1	2	2
KOSHER SALT	A PINCH	A PINCH	A PINCH	A PINCH
WHOLE MILK	2 CUPS	2 CUPS	4 CUPS	4 CUPS
HALF & HALF	1/2 CUP	1/2 CUP	1 CUP	1 CUP
GRANULATED SUGAR	1/2 CUP	1/2 CUP	1 CUP	1 CUP
RAISINS	1/3 CUP	1/3 CUP	2/3 CUP	2/3 CUP

Method:

1. *Place rice, water, vanilla, cinnamon and salt into the pressure cooker; secure lid.*
2. *Set steam vent to SEAL and timer to 6 minutes.*
3. *When cooking is complete, let pressure release naturally.*
4. *Remove and discard cinnamon sticks then add remaining ingredients and stir thoroughly.*
5. *Remove, garnish as desired and serve.*

TIP

If you prefer thicker rice pudding, let stand before eating as it will thicken considerably while it cools down.

POACHED PEARS

	5-QUART 4 SERVINGS	**6-QUART** 4 SERVINGS	**8-QUART** 6 SERVINGS	**10-QUART** 8 SERVINGS
BOSC PEARS, PEELED	4	4	6	8
RED WINE	2 CUPS	2 CUPS	3 CUPS	4 CUPS
WATER	3 CUPS	3 CUPS	4 CUPS	6 CUPS
GRANULATED SUGAR	1 CUP	1 CUP	1 1/2 CUPS	2 CUPS
LEMON ZEST AND JUICE FROM	1 LEMON	1 LEMON	1 LEMON	1 LEMON
ORANGE ZEST AND JUICE FROM	1 ORANGE	1 ORANGE	1 ORANGE	1 ORANGE
CINNAMON STICKS	2	2	3	4
KOSHER SALT	A PINCH	A PINCH	A PINCH	A PINCH

Method:

1. Place all ingredients into the pressure cooker; secure lid.
2. Set steam vent to SEAL and timer to 6 minutes.
3. When cooking is complete, let pressure release naturally.
4. Remove, garnish as desired and serve.

STEAMED GINGERBREAD CAKE

	5-QUART MAKES 1 CAKE	6-QUART MAKES 1 CAKE	8-QUART MAKES 1 CAKE	10-QUART MAKES 1 CAKE
MOLASSES	3/4 CUP	3/4 CUP	3/4 CUP	3/4 CUP
BEER (STOUT)	1/2 CUP	1/2 CUP	1/2 CUP	1/2 CUP
BAKING SODA	1/2 tsp	1/2 tsp	1/2 tsp	1/2 tsp
LARGE EGGS	2	2	2	2
GRANULATED SUGAR	3/4 CUP	3/4 CUP	3/4 CUP	3/4 CUP
LIGHT BROWN SUGAR, PACKED	1/2 CUP	1/2 CUP	1/2 CUP	1/2 CUP
VEGETABLE OIL	1/2 CUP	1/2 CUP	1/2 CUP	1/2 CUP
ALL PURPOSE FLOUR	1 1/4 CUPS	1 1/4 CUPS	1 1/4 CUPS	1 1/4 CUPS
BAKING POWDER	1 tsp	1 tsp	1 tsp	1 tsp
GROUND GINGER	2 TBSP	2 TBSP	2 TBSP	2 TBSP
GROUND CINNAMON	1 tsp	1 tsp	1 tsp	1 tsp
GROUND CLOVES	1/4 tsp	1/4 tsp	1/4 tsp	1/4 tsp
GROUND NUTMEG	1/4 tsp	1/4 tsp	1/4 tsp	1/4 tsp
GROUND CARDAMOM	1/8 tsp	1/8 tsp	1/8 tsp	1/8 tsp
KOSHER SALT	1/2 tsp	1/2 tsp	1/2 tsp	1/2 tsp
POWDERED SUGAR, FOR SERVING	AS DESIRED	AS DESIRED	AS DESIRED	AS DESIRED

TIP

Heating the molasses, beer and baking soda together is the simple but unusual step that delivers this cake's deep, rich taste.

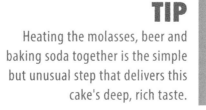

Method:

1. Combine the molasses, beer and baking soda in a saucepan over medium heat.
2. Bring to a simmer then remove and let cool to room temperature; set aside.
3. In a large mixing bowl, whisk together the eggs, granulated and brown sugars as well as oil; set aside.
4. Sift together the flour, baking powder, all of the spices and salt; set aside.
5. Whisk the cooled molasses mixture into the egg mixture then fold in the flour mixture; do not over mix.
6. Apply nonstick cooking spray to two 6" cake pans then place parchment paper inside the bottom of the pans.
7. Divide the batter evenly between the pans.
8. Place the steaming rack or a folded kitchen towel into the bottom of the pressure cooker.
9. Make a foil sling for the cake pans (see page 8).
10. Pour 2 cups of water into the pressure cooker then lower one cake pan into the pressure cooker using the foil sling; secure lid then set steam vent to VENT (you will not cook using pressure) and timer to 30 minutes.
11. When cooking is complete, carefully remove then repeat with other cake pan (add more water to pressure cooker if needed).
12. Sprinkle with powdered sugar, garnish as desired and serve.

SWEET CHILI

CHICKEN

	5-QUART 4 SERVINGS	6-QUART 4 SERVINGS	8-QUART 6 SERVINGS	10-QUART 8 SERVINGS
CHICKEN BREASTS OR THIGHS (CAN BE FROZEN)	4	4	6	8
KOSHER SALT AND FRESH PEPPER	TO TASTE	TO TASTE	TO TASTE	TO TASTE
CHICKEN STOCK	1/2 CUP	1/2 CUP	3/4 CUP	1 CUP
SWEET CHILI SAUCE, BOTTLED	1/2 CUP	1/2 CUP	3/4 CUP	1 CUP
SOY SAUCE, BOTTLED	TO TASTE	TO TASTE	TO TASTE	TO TASTE

Method:

1. *Place all ingredients into the pressure cooker; secure lid.*
2. *Set steam vent to SEAL and timer to 8 minutes.*
3. *When cooking is complete, let pressure release naturally.*
4. *Remove, garnish as desired and serve.*

RECIPES

TIP

This dish is great served with the brown rice on page 58.

SOFT OR HARD
BOILED EGGS

	5-QUART MAKES 8 EGGS	6-QUART MAKES 10 EGGS	8-QUART MAKES 12 EGGS	10-QUART MAKES 16 EGGS
LARGE EGGS	8	10	12	16
WATER	1/4 CUP	1/4 CUP	1/4 CUP	1/4 CUP

Method:

1. *Place eggs and water into the pressure cooker; secure lid.*
2. *Set steam vent to SEAL and timer to 4 minutes for soft boiled eggs or 5 minutes for hard boiled eggs.*
3. *Monitor cooker carefully and as soon as cooking is complete, immediately release the pressure manually (see tips on page 7) then remove lid.*
4. *For soft boiled eggs, remove and serve immediately.*
5. *For hard boiled eggs, remove cooking pot then run cold water over eggs.*
6. *Crack the eggs all over against the side of the cooking pot then peel eggs while hot under the running water (the water stream helps remove the shell).*
7. *Serve as desired.*

TIP

The exact cooking time is critical to achieve perfectly cooked eggs. Use a separate timer on your phone to monitor the time precisely if desired. Also, you can make any number of eggs using 1/4 cup water as long as it does not exceed the MAX line of the removable cooking pot.

NO FUSS
CABBAGE ROLLS

	5-QUART 4-5 SERVINGS	6-QUART 4-5 SERVINGS	8-QUART 6-8 SERVINGS	10-QUART 6-8 SERVINGS
GREEN CABBAGE, SLICED	5 CUPS	5 CUPS	10 CUPS	10 CUPS
CANNED TOMATO PUREE (14 OZ SIZE)	1 CAN	1 CAN	2 CANS	2 CANS
YELLOW MUSTARD	1 TBSP	1 TBSP	2 TBSP	2 TBSP
DRY MUSTARD POWDER	2 tsp	2 tsp	4 tsp	4 tsp
ALL PURPOSE FLOUR OR CORNSTARCH	1 TBSP	1 TBSP	2 TBSP	2 TBSP
GRANULATED SUGAR	1/3 CUP	1/3 CUP	2/3 CUP	2/3 CUP
APPLE CIDER VINEGAR	3 TBSP	3 TBSP	1/3 CUP	1/3 CUP
KOSHER SALT AND FRESH PEPPER	TO TASTE	TO TASTE	TO TASTE	TO TASTE
BULK BREAKFAST SAUSAGE WITH SAGE, RAW	1 POUND	1 POUND	2 POUNDS	2 POUNDS
YELLOW ONION, SMALL, CHOPPED	1	1	2	2
RICE, COOKED	1 CUP	1 CUP	2 CUPS	2 CUPS
KETCHUP	1/2 CUP	1/2 CUP	1 CUP	1 CUP
LARGE EGG	1	1	2	2
BEEF-FLAVORED BASE, STORE-BOUGHT	2 tsp	2 tsp	4 tsp	4 tsp

Method:

1. *Place the cabbage into the pressure cooker; set aside.*
2. *In a mixing bowl, whisk together the tomato puree, mustard, mustard powder, flour, sugar, vinegar, salt and pepper until smooth; set aside.*
3. *In a separate bowl, stir together the sausage, onions, rice, ketchup, egg and beef base.*
4. *Pat the sausage mixture on top of the cabbage inside the pressure cooker.*
5. *Pour tomato mixture over pressure cooker contents. Pull sausage mixture back using a fork to ensure that most of it flows over the cabbage; secure lid.*
6. *Set steam vent to SEAL and timer to 20 minutes.*
7. *When cooking is complete, let pressure release naturally.*
8. *Remove, garnish as desired and serve.*

TIP

This recipe is a breeze to prepare compared to the traditional method. It is layered instead of rolled but the delicious flavors still taste like you've been cooking for hours.

PIZZA STYLE CHICKEN BREASTS

	5-QUART 4 SERVINGS	6-QUART 5 SERVINGS	8-QUART 6 SERVINGS	10-QUART 7 SERVINGS
CHICKEN STOCK	1/2 CUP	2/3 CUP	3/4 CUP	1 CUP
BONELESS, SKINLESS CHICKEN BREASTS (CAN BE FROZEN)	4	5	6	7
PASTA SAUCE, JARRED	1 1/2 CUPS	1 2/3 CUPS	2 1/4 CUPS	3 CUPS
PEPPERONI SLICES	16	20	24	32
MOZZARELLA CHEESE, SHREDDED	1/2 CUP	2/3 CUP	3/4 CUP	1 CUP
KOSHER SALT AND FRESH PEPPER	TO TASTE	TO TASTE	TO TASTE	TO TASTE

Method:

1. *Place all ingredients in the order listed into the pressure cooker, keeping the pepperoni slices and cheese on top of the chicken breasts; secure lid.*
2. *Set steam vent to SEAL and timer to 8 minutes.*
3. *When cooking is complete, let pressure release naturally.*
4. *Remove, garnish as desired and serve.*

TIP

This recipe is great served with the easiest buttered noodles on page 63.

PORK ROAST WITH
APPLE BUTTER

	5-QUART 3-4 SERVINGS	6-QUART 4-5 SERVINGS	8-QUART 5-6 SERVINGS	10-QUART 6-7 SERVINGS
PORK SHOULDER	2 1/2 POUNDS	3 POUNDS	4 1/2 POUNDS	6 POUNDS
KOSHER SALT AND FRESH PEPPER	TO TASTE	TO TASTE	TO TASTE	TO TASTE
APPLE JUICE	1 1/2 CUPS	2 CUPS	3 CUPS	4 CUPS
APPLE BUTTER, JARRED, DIVIDED	1 1/2 CUPS	1 3/4 CUPS	2 1/4 CUPS	2 2/3 CUPS

Method:

1. *Place pork, salt, pepper, apple juice and half of the apple butter into the pressure cooker; set remaining apple butter aside then secure lid.*
2. *Set steam vent to SEAL and timer to 40 minutes.*
3. *When cooking is complete, let pressure release naturally.*
4. *Slice pork, garnish as desired and serve with remaining apple butter.*

POTATO SALAD

RECIPES

	5-QUART 3-4 SERVINGS	6-QUART 4-5 SERVINGS	8-QUART 5-6 SERVINGS	10-QUART 6-7 SERVINGS
RED POTATOES, SMALL, UNPEELED	2 POUNDS	2 1/2 POUNDS	3 1/4 POUNDS	4 POUNDS
CHICKEN STOCK	1/2 CUP	2/3 CUP	3/4 CUP	1 CUP
APPLE CIDER VINEGAR	2 TBSP	2 1/2 TBSP	3 TBSP	1/4 CUP
KOSHER SALT AND FRESH PEPPER	TO TASTE	TO TASTE	TO TASTE	TO TASTE
YELLOW ONION, MEDIUM, DICED	1	1 1/4	1 3/4	2
CELERY STALKS, DICED	3	4	5	6
LARGE DILL PICKLE, DICED	1	1 1/4	1 3/4	2
SWEET GHERKINS, DICED	4	5	6	8
MAYONNAISE	AS DESIRED	AS DESIRED	AS DESIRED	AS DESIRED
YELLOW MUSTARD	2 TBSP	2 1/2 TBSP	3 TBSP	1/4 CUP
WORCESTERSHIRE SAUCE, BOTTLED	2 tsp	2 tsp	1 TBSP	1 1/4 TBSP
HARD BOILED EGGS, SLICED, OPTIONAL (SEE PAGE 79)	3	4	5	6
PARSLEY, CHOPPED, FOR SERVING	AS DESIRED	AS DESIRED	AS DESIRED	AS DESIRED

Method:

1. *Place potatoes, stock, vinegar, salt and pepper into the pressure cooker; secure lid.*
2. *Set steam vent to SEAL and timer to 6 minutes.*
3. *When cooking is complete, let pressure release naturally.*
4. *Slice, dice or quarter potatoes while still hot into a large mixing bowl then pour 3 tablespoons of the cooking liquid from inside the pressure cooker over the potatoes; toss gently until absorbed then let cool.*
5. *Stir in remaining ingredients, using as much mayonnaise as desired to make the potato salad bind together.*
6. *Garnish as desired and serve.*

TIP

When you pour the seasoned cooking liquid over the cut potatoes in step 4, it fully seasons the potatoes, greatly reducing the need for excess mayonnaise.

SPAGHETTI

SQUASH

	5-QUART 3-4 SERVINGS	6-QUART 3-4 SERVINGS	8-QUART 5-6 SERVINGS	10-QUART 5-6 SERVINGS
LARGE SPAGHETTI SQUASH, HALVED AND CLEANED	1	1	2	2
OLIVE OIL (OPTIONAL)	1 TBSP	1 TBSP	2 TBSP	2 TBSP
KOSHER SALT AND FRESH PEPPER	TO TASTE	TO TASTE	TO TASTE	TO TASTE
WATER	1/2 CUP	1/2 CUP	1/2 CUP	1/2 CUP

Method:

1. Place all ingredients into the pressure cooker; secure lid.
2. Set steam vent to SEAL and timer to 6 minutes.
3. When cooking is complete, let pressure release naturally.
4. Hold squash halves in a folded towel or potholder then fluff into strands using a fork.
5. Garnish as desired and serve.

SWEET & SOUR
SPARE RIBS

	5-QUART 3-4 SERVINGS	6-QUART 4-5 SERVINGS	8-QUART 5-6 SERVINGS	10-QUART 6-7 SERVINGS
KOSHER SALT AND FRESH PEPPER	TO TASTE	TO TASTE	TO TASTE	TO TASTE
PINEAPPLE CHUNKS	1 CUP	1 CUP	1 1/2 CUPS	2 CUPS
YELLOW ONION, MEDIUM, CUBED	1	1	1 1/2	2
BELL PEPPER, CUBED	1	1	1 1/2	2
PINEAPPLE JUICE	1 1/2 CUPS	1 1/2 CUPS	2 CUPS	3 CUPS
KETCHUP	1/2 CUP	1/2 CUP	3/4 CUP	1 CUP
APPLE CIDER VINEGAR	1/4 CUP	1/4 CUP	1/3 CUP	1/2 CUP
GRANULATED SUGAR	1/3 CUP	1/3 CUP	1/2 CUP	2/3 CUP
CORNSTARCH	2 TBSP	2 TBSP	3 TBSP	1/4 CUP
BABY BACK SPARE RIBS	2 SLABS	3 SLABS	4 SLABS	5 SLABS

Method:

1. *Place all ingredients, except ribs, into the pressure cooker; stir thoroughly to dissolve sugar and cornstarch.*
2. *Add ribs to the pressure cooker (curl to make ribs fit if needed) then secure lid.*
3. *Set steam vent to SEAL and timer to 25 minutes.*
4. *When cooking is complete, let pressure release naturally.*
5. *Remove, garnish as desired and serve.*

MICROWAVE CARAMEL

	5-QUART 4-6 SERVINGS	6-QUART 4-6 SERVINGS	8-QUART 4-6 SERVINGS	10-QUART 4-6 SERVINGS
GRANULATED SUGAR	1/2 CUP	1/2 CUP	1/2 CUP	1/2 CUP
LIGHT CORN SYRUP	1/4 CUP	1/4 CUP	1/4 CUP	1/4 CUP
LEMON JUICE	1/4 tsp	1/4 tsp	1/4 tsp	1/4 tsp

Method:

1. *Combine all ingredients in a microwave-safe 4-cup glass measuring cup; stir until all of the sugar is moistened.*

2. *Place measuring cup with sugar mixture in the microwave then cook on high for 2-3 minutes or until bubbles start piling up on top of each other (time may vary depending on your microwave).*

3. *Continue cooking and monitoring mixture until it turns amber in color then carefully remove and let it sit for 30 seconds (color deepens as it sits).*

4. *Quickly use caramel as desired before it hardens. Use caution as mixture is extremely hot.*

TIP

You can make pretty, edible decorations with any extra microwave caramel by swirling a lacy pattern from a caramel-dipped fork onto parchment paper. This recipe is also great for caramelized sugar on top of Crème Brûlée if you do not have a blowtorch.

RECIPES

TERIYAKI
CHICKEN WINGS

	5-QUART 3-4 SERVINGS	6-QUART 4-5 SERVINGS	8-QUART 5-6 SERVINGS	10-QUART 6-7 SERVINGS
CHICKEN WINGS (CAN BE FROZEN)	16	18	24	32
SOY SAUCE, BOTTLED	TO TASTE	TO TASTE	TO TASTE	TO TASTE
CHICKEN STOCK	1 CUP	1 CUP	1 1/2 CUPS	2 CUPS
TERIYAKI SAUCE (14 OZ SIZE BOTTLE)	1 BOTTLE	1 BOTTLE	1 1/2 BOTTLES	2 BOTTLES
SESAME SEEDS	1 TBSP	1 TBSP	1 1/2 TBSP	2 TBSP

Method:

1. *Place all ingredients, except sesame seeds, into the pressure cooker; secure lid.*
2. *Set steam vent to SEAL and timer to 10 minutes.*
3. *When cooking is complete, let pressure release naturally.*
4. *Remove, garnish as desired and serve topped with sesame seeds.*

TUNA CASSEROLE

	5-QUART 3-4 SERVINGS	6-QUART 3-4 SERVINGS	8-QUART 5-6 SERVINGS	10-QUART 6-7 SERVINGS
PASTA, SMALL, DRY	1 CUP	1 CUP	1 1/2 CUPS	2 CUPS
CHICKEN STOCK	1 CUP	1 CUP	1 1/2 CUPS	2 CUPS
TUNA IN WATER OR OIL (5 OZ SIZE CAN), UN-DRAINED	1 CAN	1 CAN	2 CANS	3 CANS
BUTTER, UNSALTED	1 TBSP	1 TBSP	2 TBSP	3 TBSP
YELLOW ONION, MEDIUM, CHOPPED	1	1	1 1/2	2
WATER CHESTNUTS, DICED (5 SIZE CAN), DRAINED	1	1	1 1/2	2
CELERY STALKS, SLICED	2	2	3	4
CARROTS, SLICED	2	2	3	4
KOSHER SALT AND FRESH PEPPER	TO TASTE	TO TASTE	TO TASTE	TO TASTE
CHEDDAR CHEESE, SHREDDED	2/3 CUP	2/3 CUP	1 CUP	1 1/3 CUPS
CHOW MEIN NOODLES, CANNED	1/2 CUP	1/2 CUP	3/4 CUP	1 CUP

Method:

1. *Place all ingredients, except chow mein noodles, into the pressure cooker; stir well then secure lid.*
2. *Set steam vent to SEAL and timer to 6 minutes.*
3. *When cooking is complete, let pressure release naturally.*
4. *Remove, garnish as desired and serve topped with chow mein noodles.*

TIP

I grew up eating a more complicated version of this dish. This modern version is so easy, it creates only one pot to wash and uses only ingredients I almost always have on hand. Sometimes i even make it with a vegetarian meat substitute you can find in the freezer section of your supermarket.

RECIPES

90

KUNG PAO
RAMEN

	5-QUART 3-4 SERVINGS	6-QUART 3-4 SERVINGS	8-QUART 4-5 SERVINGS	10-QUART 5-6 SERVINGS
MEDIUM SHRIMP, PEELED AND DEVEINED	1 POUND	1 POUND	1 1/2 POUNDS	2 POUNDS
OLIVE OIL	2 TBSP	2 TBSP	3 TBSP	1/4 CUP
KOSHER SALT AND FRESH PEPPER	TO TASTE	TO TASTE	TO TASTE	TO TASTE
GARLIC CLOVES, CHOPPED	2	2	3	4
FRESH GINGER, CHOPPED	2 tsp	2 tsp	2 1/2 tsp	1 TBSP
RED BELL PEPPER, SLICED	1	1	1 1/2	2
CHILI FLAKES	TO TASTE	TO TASTE	TO TASTE	TO TASTE
HONEY	1 TBSP	1 TBSP	1 1/2 TBSP	2 TBSP
RICE VINEGAR	1 TBSP	1 TBSP	1 1/2 TBSP	2 TBSP
WATER	3 CUPS	3 CUPS	4 1/2 CUPS	6 CUPS
HOISIN SAUCE, BOTTLED	2 TBSP	2 TBSP	3 TBSP	1/4 CUP
RAMEN NOODLES (3 OZ EACH) WITH SEASONING PACKET	2	2	3	4
GREEN ONIONS, SLICED, FOR SERVING	AS DESIRED	AS DESIRED	AS DESIRED	AS DESIRED

Method:

1. Set timer to 2 minutes and let pressure cooker preheat for 5 minutes with the lid off.
2. In a bowl, toss shrimp with salt and pepper.
3. Add the oil to the pressure cooker.
4. When oil is hot, add shrimp and cook for 2 minutes, stirring constantly then remove to a plate and set aside.
5. Place remaining ingredients into the pressure cooker; stir well then secure lid.
6. Set steam vent to SEAL and keep timer set to 2 minutes.
7. When cooking is complete, carefully release the pressure manually (see tips on page 7) then remove lid.
8. Stir reserved shrimp into the noodle mixture, garnish as desired and serve.

TIP

Use this recipe template to create easy ramen from what you have on hand. I've used tofu or vegetarian meat substitute and have loved it. It is also a great recipe to use leftover vegetables.

EASIEST CHICKEN BREAST
EVER

	5-QUART 3 SERVINGS	6-QUART 4 SERVINGS	8-QUART 5 SERVINGS	10-QUART 6 SERVINGS
CHICKEN BREASTS (CAN BE FROZEN)	3	4	5	6
KOSHER SALT AND FRESH PEPPER	TO TASTE	TO TASTE	TO TASTE	TO TASTE
CHICKEN STOCK OR WATER	1 CUP	1 1/4 CUPS	1 2/3 CUPS	2 CUPS
THOUSAND ISLAND DRESSING, BOTTLED	1/3 CUP	1/2 CUP	1/2 CUP	2/3 CUP
POTATO CHIPS, CRUSHED	1/3 CUP	1/2 CUP	1/2 CUP	2/3 CUP

Method:

1. Season each chicken breast with salt and pepper.
2. Pour stock or water into the pressure cooker then add the chicken.
3. Top each chicken breast with a spoonful of dressing then secure lid.
4. Set steam vent to SEAL and timer to 8 minutes.
5. When cooking is complete, let pressure release naturally.
6. Top with some crushed potato chips for added crunch, garnish as desired and serve.

TIP
You can make this same dish using pork chops instead of chicken.

CURRIED CAULIFLOWER SOUP

	5-QUART 4-5 SERVINGS	6-QUART 5-6 SERVINGS	8-QUART 6-7 SERVINGS	10-QUART 7-8 SERVINGS
CAULIFLOWER FLORETS, FRESH OR FROZEN	4 CUPS	4 1/2 CUPS	6 CUPS	8 CUPS
VEGETABLE STOCK	1 CUP	1 1/4 CUPS	1 3/4 CUPS	2 CUPS
COCONUT OIL	3 TBSP	3 TBSP	1/4 CUP	1/4 CUP
COCONUT MILK	3 CUPS	4 CUPS	5 CUPS	6 CUPS
YELLOW ONION, LARGE, CHOPPED	1	1 1/4	1 3/4	2
GARLIC CLOVES, CHOPPED	4	4	6	8
FRESH GINGER, CHOPPED	1 TBSP	1 1/4 TBSP	1 1/2 TBSP	2 TBSP
CURRY POWDER OR GARAM MASALA	2 TBSP	2 1/4 TBSP	3 TBSP	1/4 CUP
GRANULATED SUGAR OR HONEY	1 TBSP	1 1/4 TBSP	1 3/4 TBSP	2 TBSP
CILANTRO	2 TBSP	2 1/2 TBSP	3 TBSP	1/4 CUP
FRESH LIME JUICE	2 TBSP	2 TBSP	3 TBSP	1/4 CUP
KOSHER SALT AND FRESH PEPPER	TO TASTE	TO TASTE	TO TASTE	TO TASTE
FRESH HOT CHILIES OR CHILI FLAKES	TO TASTE	TO TASTE	TO TASTE	TO TASTE

Method:

1. Place all ingredients into the pressure cooker; secure lid.
2. Set steam vent to SEAL and timer to 6 minutes.
3. When cooking is complete, let pressure release naturally.
4. Garnish as desired and serve.

TIP

For a smoother soup, use an immersion blender right inside the pressure cooker after cooking until desired consistency is achieved.

EASY
CHICKEN WINGS

	5-QUART 3-4 SERVINGS	6-QUART 4-5 SERVINGS	8-QUART 6-7 SERVINGS	10-QUART 7-8 SERVINGS
CHICKEN WINGS, RAW (CAN BE FROZEN)	16	18	24	32
CHICKEN STOCK	1/3 CUP	1/3 CUP	1/2 CUP	2/3 CUP
BUFFALO WING SAUCE, BOTTLED	1 CUP	1 CUP	1 1/2 CUPS	2 CUPS
KOSHER SALT AND FRESH PEPPER	TO TASTE	TO TASTE	TO TASTE	TO TASTE
BLUE CHEESE CRUMBLES	AS DESIRED	AS DESIRED	AS DESIRED	AS DESIRED
CELERY STICKS, FOR SERVING	AS DESIRED	AS DESIRED	AS DESIRED	AS DESIRED

Method:

1. *Place all ingredients, except blue cheese and celery, into the pressure cooker.*
2. *Stir pressure cooker contents thoroughly until wings are well coated with sauce; secure lid.*
3. *Set steam vent to SEAL and timer to 9 minutes.*
4. *When cooking is complete, carefully release the pressure manually (see tips on page 7) then remove lid.*
5. *Serve as desired with blue cheese and celery sticks.*

TIP

Don't like bones or skin? Use
chicken breasts or chicken tenders.

MEXICAN CORN

	5-QUART 4 SERVINGS	6-QUART 5 SERVINGS	8-QUART 7 SERVINGS	10-QUART 8 SERVINGS
EARS OF CORN, SHUCKED (HALVED IF NEEDED)	4	5	7	8
WATER	1/4 CUP	1/4 CUP	1/4 CUP	1/4 CUP
ANCHO CHILE POWDER + MORE FOR SERVING	2 tsp	2 1/2 tsp	3 tsp	4 tsp
LIME JUICE + MORE FOR SERVING	2 TBSP	2 1/2 TBSP	3 TBSP	4 TBSP
KOSHER SALT	TO TASTE	TO TASTE	TO TASTE	TO TASTE
MAYONNAISE	AS DESIRED	AS DESIRED	AS DESIRED	AS DESIRED
PARMESAN CHEESE, GRATED OR QUESO FRESCO	AS DESIRED	AS DESIRED	AS DESIRED	AS DESIRED

Method:

1. *Place all ingredients, except mayonnaise and cheese, into the pressure cooker; secure lid.*
2. *Set steam vent to SEAL and timer to 2 minutes.*
3. *When cooking is complete, carefully release the pressure manually (see tips on page 7) then remove lid.*
4. *Spread mayonnaise on the corn then sprinkle with cheese and additional lime juice as well as chile powder.*

HOMEMADE
CHICKEN STOCK

	5-QUART MAKES 1 1/2 QUARTS	6-QUART MAKES 1 1/2 QUARTS	8-QUART MAKES 3 QUARTS	10-QUART MAKES 3 QUARTS
OLIVE OIL	2 TBSP	2 TBSP	1/4 CUP	1/4 CUP
WHOLE CHICKEN WINGS, RAW	1 1/2 POUNDS	1 1/2 POUNDS	3 POUNDS	3 POUNDS
YELLOW ONION, LARGE, ROUGHLY CHOPPED	1	1	2	2
CARROT, ROUGHLY CHOPPED	1	1	2	2
CELERY STALK, ROUGHLY CHOPPED	1	1	2	2
PEPPERCORNS	6	6	12	12
THYME SPRIG	1	1	2	2
WATER, COLD	AS NEEDED	AS NEEDED	AS NEEDED	AS NEEDED

Method:

1. *Set timer to 30 minutes and let pressure cooker preheat for 5 minutes with the lid off.*
2. *Add the oil to the pressure cooker.*
3. *When oil is hot, add the wings and brown them on both sides for a total of 15 minutes.*
4. *Place remaining ingredients into the pressure cooker then add cold water until 1" below the MAX line; secure lid.*
5. *Set steam vent to SEAL and keep timer set to 30 minutes.*
6. *When cooking is complete, let pressure release naturally.*
7. *Remove lid then strain stock and discard solids.*
8. *Use as desired or freeze for up to 3 months.*

RANCH ONION
CHICKEN

	5-QUART 4 SERVINGS	6-QUART 5 SERVINGS	8-QUART 6 SERVINGS	10-QUART 8 SERVINGS
CHICKEN BREASTS OR THIGHS (CAN BE FROZEN)	4	5	6	8
FRESH PEPPER	TO TASTE	TO TASTE	TO TASTE	TO TASTE
PEARL ONIONS, FROZEN (10 OZ SIZE BAG)	1 BAG	1 BAG	1 1/2 BAGS	2 BAGS
RANCH MIX (.75 OZ SIZE PACKET)	1 PACKET	1 PACKET	1 1/2 PACKETS	2 PACKETS
CORNSTARCH OR ALL PURPOSE FLOUR	1 TBSP	1 TBSP	1 1/2 TBSP	2 TBSP
MILK	1 CUP	1 1/4 CUPS	1 2/3 CUPS	2 CUPS
FRENCH FRIED ONION RINGS, CANNED	1 CUP	1 CUP	1 1/2 CUPS	2 CUPS

Method:

1. *Place all ingredients, except French fried onion rings, into the pressure cooker; stir well then secure lid.*
2. *Set steam vent to SEAL and timer to 8 minutes.*
3. *When cooking is complete, let pressure release naturally.*
4. *Remove, garnish as desired then top with French fried onion rings before serving.*

BANANA
BREAD PUDDING

	5-QUART 4-6 SERVINGS	6-QUART 4-6 SERVINGS	8-QUART 6-7 SERVINGS	10-QUART 7-8 SERVINGS
HEAVY CREAM OR HALF & HALF	2 CUPS	2 CUPS	3 CUPS	4 CUPS
LARGE EGGS	6	6	9	12
BROWN SUGAR, PACKED	1/2 CUP	1/2 CUP	3/4 CUP	1 CUP
VANILLA EXTRACT	2 tsp	2 tsp	1 TBSP	1 1/2 TBSP
LEMON JUICE, FRESH	2 tsp	2 tsp	1 TBSP	1 1/2 TBSP
KOSHER SALT	A PINCH	A PINCH	A PINCH	A PINCH
VERY RIPE BANANAS, SLICED	2	2	3	4
TOASTED PECANS (OPTIONAL)	1/4 CUP	1/4 CUP	1/3 CUP	1/2 CUP
BREAD CUBES, SUCH AS CHALLAH	3 CUPS	3 CUPS	4 CUPS	6 CUPS
POWDERED SUGAR, FOR SERVING	AS DESIRED	AS DESIRED	AS DESIRED	AS DESIRED

Method:

1. *Apply nonstick spray to the pressure cooker.*
2. *In a large bowl, whisk together all ingredients, except banana slices, pecans, bread and powdered sugar.*
3. *Add the banana slices, pecans and bread then gently press down to help bread absorb the liquid.*
4. *Pour mixture into the pressure cooker; secure lid.*
5. *Set steam vent to SEAL and timer to 20 minutes.*
6. *When cooking is complete, let pressure release naturally.*
7. *Remove, top with powdered sugar, garnish as desired and serve.*

EASY
ARTICHOKES

	5-QUART 3-4 SERVINGS	6-QUART 4-5 SERVINGS	8-QUART 5-6 SERVINGS	10-QUART 6-8 SERVINGS
LARGE GLOBE ARTICHOKES	2	3	4	6
LEMON SLICES	4	4	4	6
KOSHER SALT	TO TASTE	TO TASTE	TO TASTE	TO TASTE
WATER	1 CUP	1 CUP	1 CUP	1 CUP

Method:

1. Cut off stems evenly so that artichokes can sit flat while cooking.
2. Place all ingredients into the pressure cooker; secure lid.
3. Set steam vent to SEAL and timer to 12 minutes.
4. When cooking is complete, let pressure release naturally.
5. Remove, garnish as desired and serve.

RECIPES

TIP

For a simple yet delicious dipping sauce, stir together 2 tablespoons each liquid from the artichokes, mayonnaise and bottled sweet chili sauce.

HONEY MUSTARD
CHICKEN

	5-QUART 3-4 SERVINGS	6-QUART 4-5 SERVINGS	8-QUART 5-6 SERVINGS	10-QUART 6-7 SERVINGS
CHICKEN PIECES OF YOUR CHOICE	3/4 POUND	1 POUND	2 POUNDS	3 POUNDS
BUTTER, UNSALTED	1/2 TBSP	1 TBSP	2 TBSP	3 TBSP
YELLOW ONION, MEDIUM, SLICED	1	1	2	3
WHOLE GRAIN MUSTARD	2 TBSP	3 TBSP	1/4 CUP	1/2 CUP
HONEY	3 TBSP	3 TBSP	1/4 CUP	1/3 CUP
KOSHER SALT AND FRESH PEPPER	TO TASTE	TO TASTE	TO TASTE	TO TASTE
CHICKEN STOCK	2/3 CUP	1 CUP	1 1/4 CUPS	1 1/2 CUPS
WORCESTERSHIRE SAUCE, BOTTLED	1 tsp	2 tsp	1 TBSP	1 1/2 TBSP
CORNSTARCH	1/2 TBSP	1 TBSP	2 TBSP	3 TBSP

Method:

1. *Place all ingredients into the pressure cooker; stir well then secure lid.*
2. *Set steam vent to SEAL and timer to 15 minutes.*
3. *When cooking is complete, let pressure release naturally.*
4. *Garnish as desired and serve.*

CHICKEN NOODLE SOUP

	5-QUART 3-4 SERVINGS	6-QUART 4-5 SERVINGS	8-QUART 6-7 SERVINGS	10-QUART 7-8 SERVINGS
CHICKEN PIECES (CAN BE FROZEN)	1 POUND	1 1/4 POUNDS	1 3/4 POUNDS	2 POUNDS
YELLOW ONION, LARGE, CHOPPED	1	1 1/4	1 3/4	2
CELERY, CHOPPED	1 CUP	1 1/4 CUPS	1 3/4 CUPS	2 CUPS
CARROT, CHOPPED	2 CUPS	2 1/4 CUPS	3 CUPS	4 CUPS
BAY LEAF	1	1	2	2
CHICKEN STOCK	6 CUPS	8 CUPS	10 CUPS	12 CUPS
KOSHER SALT AND FRESH PEPPER	TO TASTE	TO TASTE	TO TASTE	TO TASTE
DRIED SAGE	1/4 tsp	1/2 tsp	3/4 tsp	1 tsp
EGG NOODLES, DRY	2 CUPS	2 1/4 CUPS	3 CUPS	4 CUPS
PARSLEY, CHOPPED, FOR SERVING	1 TBSP	1 TBSP	2 TBSP	2 TBSP

Method:

1. *Place all ingredients, except parsley, into the pressure cooker; secure lid.*
2. *Set steam vent to SEAL and timer to 15 minutes.*
3. *When cooking is complete, let pressure release naturally.*
4. *Remove, garnish as desired and serve topped with parsley.*

TIP

For firmer noodles, add them after pressure cooking is complete. Turn on pressure cooker to let soup simmer by setting the timer but leaving the lid off. Let noodles cook for 5 minutes before serving soup.

CILANTRO LIME
CHICKEN

	5-QUART 3-4 SERVINGS	6-QUART 4-5 SERVINGS	8-QUART 5-6 SERVINGS	10-QUART 6-7 SERVINGS
CHICKEN THIGHS OR BREASTS (CAN BE FROZEN)	1 POUND	1 1/2 POUNDS	1 3/4 POUNDS	2 POUNDS
CHICKEN STOCK	1 1/2 CUPS	2 CUPS	2 1/2 CUPS	3 CUPS
GARLIC CLOVES, CHOPPED	6	8	10	12
MEXICAN SEASONING	1 TBSP	1 1/4 TBSP	1 3/4 TBSP	2 TBSP
WHITE ONION, LARGE, SLICED	2	2 1/2	3	4
OLIVE OIL	3 TBSP	3 TBSP	4 TBSP	4 TBSP
LIME JUICE + MORE FOR SERVING	1/4 CUP	1/4 CUP	1/3 CUP	1/2 CUP
CILANTRO + MORE FOR SERVING	1/4 CUP	1/4 CUP	1/3 CUP	1/2 CUP
KOSHER SALT	TO TASTE	TO TASTE	TO TASTE	TO TASTE

Method:

1. *Place all ingredients into the pressure cooker; secure lid.*
2. *Set steam vent to SEAL and timer to 8 minutes.*
3. *When cooking is complete, let pressure release naturally.*
4. *Garnish with additional lime and cilantro before serving.*

TIP

As an alternative, use pork shoulder or tenderloin instead of chicken.

COOK
ANY BEAN

	5-QUART	6-QUART	8-QUART	10-QUART	COOKING TIME
WATER	8 CUPS	8 CUPS	12 CUPS	16 CUPS	
DARK RED KIDNEY BEANS	2 CUPS	2 CUPS	3 CUPS	4 CUPS	15 MIN
PINTO BEANS	2 CUPS	2 CUPS	3 CUPS	4 CUPS	15 MIN
BLACK BEANS	2 CUPS	2 CUPS	3 CUPS	4 CUPS	12 MIN
NAVY BEANS	2 CUPS	2 CUPS	3 CUPS	4 CUPS	8 MIN
GREAT NORTHERN BEANS	2 CUPS	2 CUPS	3 CUPS	4 CUPS	15 MIN
BLACK EYED PEAS	2 CUPS	2 CUPS	3 CUPS	4 CUPS	12 MIN
SPLIT PEAS	2 CUPS	2 CUPS	3 CUPS	4 CUPS	6 MIN
LENTILS	2 CUPS	2 CUPS	3 CUPS	4 CUPS	6 MIN
DRIED LIMA BEANS	2 CUPS	2 CUPS	3 CUPS	4 CUPS	15 MIN
CANNELLINI BEANS	2 CUPS	2 CUPS	3 CUPS	4 CUPS	20 MIN
CHICKPEAS	2 CUPS	2 CUPS	3 CUPS	4 CUPS	18 MIN

Method:

1. *Rinse beans thoroughly using a strainer.*
2. *Place all ingredients into the pressure cooker; secure lid.*
3. *Set steam vent to SEAL and timer according to chart above.*
4. *When cooking is complete, let pressure release naturally.*
5. *Let beans stand on KEEP WARM for a minimum of 1 hour or up to several hours.*
6. *Season beans as desired before serving.*

TIP

It is important to avoid adding salt or any acidic ingredient such as tomatoes before starting to cook as they prevent beans from becoming tender. Once they are cooked you can add seasonings as desired.

If your type of bean is not listed above, use the recipe template for the bean that is most similar in size to the one you wish to cook.

CHICKEN ENCHILADA CASSEROLE

	5-QUART 3-4 SERVINGS	6-QUART 4-5 SERVINGS	8-QUART 6-7 SERVINGS	10-QUART 7-8 SERVINGS
BONELESS CHICKEN BREASTS OR THIGHS (CAN BE FROZEN)	2	3	4	5
CHICKEN STOCK	1 CUP	1 1/2 CUPS	1 3/4 CUPS	2 CUPS
YELLOW ONION, LARGE, CHOPPED	1	1 1/4	1 1/2	2
DARK RED KIDNEY BEANS, COOKED	1 CUP	1 1/2 CUPS	1 3/4 CUPS	2 CUPS
ENCHILADA SAUCE, CANNED	1 CUP	1 1/2 CUPS	1 3/4 CUPS	2 CUPS
SALSA, JARRED	1 CUP	1 1/2 CUPS	1 3/4 CUPS	2 CUPS
TACO SEASONING	TO TASTE	TO TASTE	TO TASTE	TO TASTE
CORN KERNELS, FRESH OR CANNED	1 CUP	1 1/2 CUPS	1 3/4 CUPS	2 CUPS
TORTILLA CHIPS	2 CUPS	2 1/2 CUPS	3 CUPS	4 CUPS
CILANTRO, SOUR CREAM, JALAPEÑO PEPPERS, FOR SERVING	AS DESIRED	AS DESIRED	AS DESIRED	AS DESIRED

TIP

This casserole is equally good made with ground beef. It is also a very forgiving recipe, which is ideal for using any leftover vegetables you might have in your refrigerator.

Method:

1. *Place all ingredients, except cilantro, sour cream and jalapeño peppers, into the pressure cooker; secure lid.*
2. *Set steam vent to SEAL and timer to 8 minutes.*
3. *When cooking is complete, let pressure release naturally.*
4. *Remove, garnish as desired and serve with cilantro, sour cream and jalapeño peppers.*

INDEX

FOR ALL OF MARIAN GETZ'S
COOKBOOKS AS WELL AS
COOKWARE, APPLIANCES, CUTLERY
AND KITCHEN ACCESSORIES
BY WOLFGANG PUCK

PLEASE VISIT
HSN.COM
(KEYWORD: WOLFGANG PUCK)